To Touch the Stars

by Karen Zeinert

JAMESTOWN PUBLISHERS

a division of NTC/CONTEMPORARY PUBLISHING GROUP
Lincolnwood, Illinois USA

Cover Credits

Design: Herman Adler Design Group

Illustration: Douglass C. Klauba

Timeline: (left) Braun Brothers; (middle) Chicago Tribune Company; (right) Official U.S. Navy Photo

Photos:

pages iii, 127-131: Courtesy of the Woman's Collection at Texas Woman's University, Denton, Texas

ISBN: 0-8092-0589-0 (hardbound)
ISBN: 0-8092-0630-7 (softbound)

Published by Jamestown Publishers,
a division of NTC/Contemporary Publishing Group, Inc.,
4255 West Touhy Avenue,
Lincolnwood (Chicago), Illinois 60712-1975 U.S.A.

Overleaf: WASP trainee Ethel Meyer Finley, wearing her oversize "zoot" suit. Avenger Field, Sweetwater, Texas, 1943

Chapter 1

As I, James Edwin Erickson, looked into my bedroom mirror, I reviewed my latest scheme for the last time. I also practiced keeping a straight face, something that's not especially easy for me to do. I knew that one slipup during my sister Liz's 18th birthday celebration today, May 1, 1942, would get me into a lot of trouble. Even though I'm only 14 years old, I've already had enough of that, so pulling off this plan without getting caught is very important to me. More important, though, is the possibility that success today would make Liz happy again *and* prove that I have the makings of a great actor.

I love the theater, and I hope to become either a famous playwright or a movie star like my hero Humphrey Bogart. I saw him in his latest film, *Casablanca*, twice. I would have gone more often, but my weekly allowance just doesn't permit more than two movies a week. It costs 10 cents to see a matinee in Chippewa Falls, Wisconsin, which I think is a lot of money. Of course, each showing includes cartoons and newsreels, which, since we entered the war last year, are mostly about soldiers going off to war and bloody battles in Asia. Right now we're not doing well on the battlefield, but there isn't a single American who doesn't believe that that will change real soon.

I've noticed that ladies really go for Bogart. So hoping to attract the attention of a certain seventh-grade girl, I've memorized some of his lines, and I use them whenever I can. My favorite is "Here's looking at you, kid." Those are the exact words Bogart spoke in *Casablanca* when he gave a special salute to Ingrid Bergman.

When Mother was alive, she defended my schemes, insisting that I was just more imaginative than most boys my age. But some of my teachers, especially Miss Preston, my English teacher, think that I am too imaginative for my own good. During a parent conference in January, she actually told Father that I was a troublemaker.

The reason for the "troublemaker" label was last September's mouse incident, which Miss Preston simply refuses to forget. I had an idea for a play that I was writing, my very first mystery. I thought that a mouse running about in a roomful of people might raise such a ruckus that a thief could steal something without being noticed.

To test my theory, I turned a mouse loose in English class. As my pet-store purchase, which I nicknamed Eddie, ran around looking for some way out, Tom Knecht tried to catch the little critter. This made Eddie frantic. He zigzagged back and forth across the room with Tom hot on his trail while my classmates laughed and cheered. Most of the girls shrieked and either stood on their chairs or raised their legs high above the floor so that the mouse couldn't touch them. My experiment caused so much commotion in the room that *three* thieves could've been at work, and no one would have noticed. In short, my theory was sound.

However, there were repercussions. Miss Preston saw me jotting in my writer's notebook—a little journal that I use to record ideas for plays, especially bits of conversations that I overhear. Anyway, my note-taking—and I was writing as fast as I could—cast suspicion upon me. When Miss Preston questioned me, I confessed and then described the purpose of my experiment, which I pointed out, was perfectly harmless. I also told Miss Preston that she should have appreciated my efforts to try to develop a realistic scene. With hands on her hips, she replied that she was not the least bit appreciative. So I got a lot of detention time. I had to spend an hour washing blackboards and clapping erasers after school every day for a *whole* week.

In order to be a great actor, a man not only has to deliver his lines correctly and with feeling, he also has to look the part. To play my role to the hilt today, I have to look like an adult. So I'm wearing my Sunday best—a new tan suit, my first, which Father said I have to wear to Liz's

3

graduation next month. I didn't get the knot in my necktie just right, and I'm not sure if the blue tie is the right one to wear, but the palest stripes match my eyes, and I like the effect.

In addition, I've temporarily tamed my unruly hair, which is almost the color of my suit. I had to use a lot of hair cream to get some of the strands to stay in place, and as a result my bedroom smells like a barber shop.

When I was sure that my appearance was perfect for my role, I had but one thing left to do. I took a small poster from its hiding place, folded the sheet several times, then slipped it into the inside pocket of my jacket. It's the prop that I hope will upset a certain adult's plans. Despite my best efforts to keep a straight face, I couldn't help smiling a little at that thought as I headed downstairs.

Chapter 2

I decided to wait for our guests on the front porch. As I sat down on the top step, I realized that today was a perfect spring day, the kind that doesn't occur often in Wisconsin. Here spring is often a mix of extreme temperatures. One day is cold and the next is hot, as very different masses of air push each other back and forth in an unsettled weather pattern. Neither extreme dominated today. Instead, the air was cool, and the bright sunshine felt comfortably warm on my face. All around me shrubs and trees, even the old elms that line our street, were leafing out. I could smell freshly cut grass, damp earth, and the fragrant blue violets that run rampant near the foot of the steps.

In front of our Victorian home, the Sullivan brothers raced their bikes down Columbia Street. As usual, they were heading toward the crest of the town's west hill so that they could coast down Columbia's steep slope to the wide river valley below. With the right amount of speed, this can be a great ride, and on any other day, I'd have gladly joined them.

Wilbert Sterling, my mother's brother, and his wife, Tina, our only guests for the celebration, arrived from Chicago at three o'clock. Uncle Wilbert didn't see me as he climbed out of his car, so I remained seated and watched my opponent very carefully.

My uncle made an impressive appearance. Tall and broad-shouldered, he moved with confidence. Every silver-gray hair was in place, and his navy double-breasted suit didn't have a single wrinkle. As he walked to Aunt Tina's side of the car to open the door for her, he held out his right hand palm side down in the sun's rays, a habit of his. He always wears a ruby ring, and he likes to watch the stone sparkle in bright light.

Diabetes runs in the Sterling family. Mother's father and aunt had the disease, and a cousin was diagnosed with a borderline case four years ago. Wilbert the Perfect, as I call him behind his back, doesn't want anyone to know about the family's medical history or the fact that he himself is at high risk. This doesn't make a lot of sense to me. Why should anyone be ashamed of having diabetes?

To make sure that his medical history remains a secret and that he has the best possible advice, Uncle Wilbert has always been examined far from home by specialists at the Mayo Clinic in Rochester, Minnesota. Because my uncle usually has a dozen business deals going at any one time in several places, he purchased a Piper Cub—a PA Super Cruiser to be exact—two years ago to make it possible to get to appointments faster. He also used the Cruiser, a two-seater, to go to Rochester for examinations. Once he began to fly to the clinic and could make the trip in only a few hours, he persuaded Mother to go to Rochester for her annual exam as well.

Both my mother and uncle received pilots' licenses when they were teenagers. Mother loved to fly, and when her father died, she used part of her inheritance to buy a red-and-white Cub, a real beauty even if it wasn't a Super Cruiser. She kept the Cub at Sipple's airfield just outside Chippewa.

For some reason, my uncle didn't feel up to piloting his plane on their last return trip from Mayo, so Mother took the controls. I never understood why she decided to take off when she did, since a spring storm had been predicted to take place about halfway between Rochester and Chippewa. When they encountered the storm, according to Uncle Wilbert, Mother thought that she could fly over it. She couldn't, though, and when she hit the squall line and started to climb, she was unable to control the plane. As the Cruiser plummeted to the ground, the plane's right wing hit a telephone line, flipping the Cub upside down. Wilbert managed to pull Mother from the wreck before it burst into flames, but there was little that he could do for her. She was dead.

Since that day, he's been hanging around here a lot. He's always telling us what to do and when to do it. I don't like him or his directions very much, so I don't look forward to his visits, particularly on special days like today, which should be happy occasions.

As Uncle Wilbert and Aunt Tina, a pale, gray-haired lady dressed entirely in white, started up the sidewalk to our front door, he spotted me. I took a deep breath before rising. My drama, for better or worse—and suddenly I had doubts about the final scene—was about to begin.

"Jim," Uncle Wilbert said loudly, "how nice to see you." He forced a smile as he reached out to grip my shoulder and give me a little shake. "How is everyone?"

"Fine. We're all fine," I replied nervously. Then I took hold of myself. "We're happy that you could be here," I said in the deepest voice that I could muster, believing that it would make me sound more mature. "Please come in. I'll tell Liz and Father that you're here."

Liz was just coming down the stairs when we entered the front hall. I know I'm biased, but I think that Liz is really pretty—or at least she would be if I could get her to smile again. She has shoulder-length blond hair, which she curls under into what I think is known as a pageboy; incredibly dark blue eyes; rosy cheeks; and a trim figure.

When Mother died, Liz kind of died too. She dropped out of all organizations and activities at school, including cheerleading—even though she would have been the captain of Chi Hi's squad this year. Now she just goes to her classes, most of the time half-halfheartedly.

Liz doesn't socialize anymore, either. Before Mother's death, Liz attended every school function: ball games; pep rallies; dances; concerts; and plays, some of which she saw several times. This year, she didn't go to one event. She also gave Bernie Levine his class ring back, insisting that she no longer wanted to go steady with him or anyone else for that matter.

And she doesn't spend much time with me. We used to join the neighborhood kids in a ball game now and then. Liz hits a softball harder than anyone I know, and she steals bases like a pro. We also used to ride our bikes for hours, especially if there was a lot of homework to do. We'd go to Irvine Park or head out of town to talk to Joe Sipple at the airfield or even ride back into the apple orchards in the hills east of town. Now she spends most of her time in her room. I know that she is still grieving over Mother's death, but once in a while I wonder if—no, I *know*—that something else is bothering her. She seems so puzzled, as if she's trying to solve a mystery but can't.

Liz hesitated briefly when she saw our guests, pushed up the sleeves of her new pink dress, then ran downstairs to hug our aunt and uncle. "Thank you for coming," she said softly. "How . . ."

I didn't hear the rest. I walked down the hall to the den, pushed open the door, and saw a familiar scene before me: Father hard at work. He is the editor of the only newspaper in town, the *Chippewa Telegram*. His job has always been demanding, but lately he's worked harder than ever, in part, I suspect, so that he doesn't think about Mother's death so often, and in part because he doesn't have enough help. As soon as we entered the war,

Mr. Littel, one of Father's two reporters, quit. He went to New York to try to find a newspaper that would send him to Europe to cover the conflict, something that the *Telegram* couldn't afford to do. So far, Father hasn't found a replacement.

Then the paper's receptionist quit to take a job at Smith Controls. Smith, which is in Eau Claire, about 10 miles from here, makes timing devices for bombs for the army. The company is eager to hire as many people as it can. It even ran ads in Father's paper asking wives to think about working outside their homes for the duration of the war. Since married women are expected to be full-time homemakers, the ads raised more than a few eyebrows. Because Smith pays higher wages than the *Telegram* does and must man the plant 24 hours a day, seven days a week, it's not likely that Father will find a receptionist soon.

So Father and Miss Jones, the only reporter on the staff now, do all the work. She covers weddings and other social events, and he writes everything else and fields calls about newspapers that haven't been delivered. The rest of the time Father writes controversial editorials. He's always on one crusade or another, challenging people to think for themselves or to fight for change. Sometimes his crusades make people angry. But Father would never give up on something that he believes in. He has Williamson blood in his veins, and the Williamsons are real fighters. During the Great Depression, Pete Williamson, who is now in the army, took on a powerful industrialist, and I've heard some mighty interesting tales about what he accomplished then.

"Father?" I said softly so that I wouldn't startle him. He looked up at me, but I could tell that his mind was far away. "Our guests are here," I said, pointing toward the living room.

Father looked at the stacks of papers on his desk and sighed. "Tell them I'll be right there," he said as he removed his reading glasses and ran his hands through his thin brown hair.

The rest of the afternoon was so boring that I could actually feel my brain cells dying, one after another, as I listened to stories about Wilbert Sterling's big business deals. Even so, true to my plan, I struggled—and struggled!—to show an interest in his work.

After what seemed like an eternity, Mrs. Smallman, our neighbor, arrived. For a birthday present, she brought over Liz's favorite supper, which included a yellow-and-white marble cake topped with thick vanilla frosting, coconut, and little white candles for dessert. As Mrs. S. carved the beef roast and filled our blue-and-white serving bowls with potatoes and vegetables, I placed the dishes on our dining room table. I anticipated a tasty meal, and I was not disappointed. Even the green beans with bits of bacon were great.

When Mrs. Smallman had cleared the last of the dishes, Uncle Wilbert lit a big cigar then turned to face Liz. "Two weeks ago," Wilbert said, "I talked to your father about your future. He told me that you haven't made any plans beyond graduation, so I've taken some action." He inhaled cigar smoke and blew a perfect smoke ring before continuing. "I've paid your tuition at Mitchell Charm School in Minneapolis, one of the best in the country. I told the administrator to send you the necessary forms. And," he added with a big smile, "I also paid for the business course. Now, what do you think of that?"

Liz looked at Father, who struggled to conceal his reaction, then turned toward Uncle Wilbert. "Charm school? You want *me* to go to charm school?"

Wilbert nodded.

"Why would I want to do that?"

For some strange reason, Wilbert must have thought that Liz would be delighted with his proposal, for when she questioned him, he was clearly taken aback. He studied her for a moment, then leaned forward to reason with her. "First of all," he replied, pointing at Liz's hands (she'd been chewing her nails again), "they'd teach you how to give yourself a proper manicure. Girls need to be taught how to be ladies, Liz, how to walk, sit, style their hair, dress, and comport themselves. Your mother isn't here to help you, so I think that some kind of finishing school is necessary. Second, the staff will teach you how to become an executive secretary, a fine job for a girl.

"Now if you'd rather go to college, I'll gladly pay your tuition. Your father told me that your grades, although not the best," he muttered under his breath, "are good enough for acceptance. You need some education, Liz, that's the important thing." He paused, taking yet another puff on his cigar. "Tuition is expensive. I thought you'd appreciate my gift."

When we were numb with grief over Mother's death, Wilbert took control of our lives. He decided that Mother would be buried in the Sterling family plot in Chicago, not here. He even chose the hymns for the memorial service. Later, Wilbert decided that we needed a cleaning lady, so he hired one without even asking us how we felt about it. (We didn't like it.) Then he started appearing every week or two to check on us and give advice. We needed—and appreciated—his help last year, but not now. I knew that Liz resented Wilbert's interference as much as I did, and that she just needed a little push to finally stand up to him. So I said as sweetly as I could, "He is only trying to help, Liz, as he has been for months." *That*, I thought, *should do it*. And it did.

"Help?" she said, raising her voice. "He wants me to be a secretary with perfect nails who knows how to," she wrinkled up her nose, "comport herself. I don't want to work in an office. I'd be more miserable than I am now. How is that helping me?"

"I'm helping you by giving you some direction in your life," Wilbert replied. "You might learn to like typing and filing. At the very least, Mitchell instructors could help you get rid of some of your unladylike behaviors, like losing your temper. You'd also have an education. If you don't want to go to Mitchell, what do you want to do?"

Liz just stared at Wilbert.

"Well?"

She continued to stare.

"I asked you a question."

Now Liz had that you-asked-for-it look on her face. "Mother and I had great plans," she began, "but. . . ." Liz took a deep breath. "If I could do anything—anything at all—I would fly. Since the first day that Mother took me for a ride in her new Cub, that's all I've ever dreamed about. I want to taxi down the runway as fast as I can, to feel the takeoff in the pit of my stomach, to soar high above the earth on a sunny day and to try to touch the stars at night. I want—"

"Don't be ridiculous!" Wilbert shouted. "Look at your mother!"

That got quite a reaction. Father made a fist and glared at Wilbert in a way I didn't think Father was capable of doing. Aunt Tina began to cry, while Liz glanced at a family portrait that hung on our dining room wall. "Yes," she said softly, "look at my mother."

Even though Liz hadn't planned to do so, she gave me the perfect opening for my presentation. But since I thought a period of silence would make my role even more dramatic, I waited a bit, staring at the portrait in the meantime, recalling how much Mother loved to fly.

When I thought the time was right, I stood up. I had practiced for this moment, and even though I believed that I was ready for it, I was surprised at how much my hands shook. Still, just as I had planned, I faced Wilbert. "I had no idea," I said, trying hard to hide the fact that I had overheard Wilbert's conversation with Father two weeks ago, "that you had made plans for Liz. I have a suggestion too, a surprise for her birthday. My idea's not as grand as yours, of course, but—"

Wilbert took another puff on his cigar. "Is that so?" he said with a haughtiness that no one could have missed.

To avoid giving him any excuse for rejecting my idea due to my behavior, I presented my suggestion as politely as possible. I didn't tell Wilbert to leave my sister alone or that I had been thrashing about for two weeks to find some way to ruin his plan, which for me was the final straw, or that in desperation I had gone out to the airfield to confide in Joe Sipple. Nor did I tell Wilbert that Joe, who had a great idea, had little information about it other than what he could gather from a few phone calls and a poster. I wasn't about to admit that my plan might be little more than wishful thinking.

Instead, I said in as confident a voice as I could manage, "As everyone knows, the government's started many programs for the war effort. When Joe heard about one of them, he thought of Liz. He asked me to give this to her." I pulled the poster from my inside pocket, unfolded the sheet, and handed it to my sister.

Liz skimmed the information, then looked up at me in disbelief.

"It's true, Liz. The government's hiring female pilots to ferry planes from their manufacturers to military bases so that male pilots who are ferrying now can go to the front. Joe—"

Wilbert tore the poster from Liz's hand, read it quickly,

and threw it on the table. "This says 'experienced and licensed pilots, ready to fly any kind of aircraft,' Jim. Although Liz has had a few lessons, she is hardly experienced nor is she licensed. And she can't fly any old kind of aircraft, either. She can't even fly a Cub, let alone a bomber."

I looked him in the eye, man to man, continuing as if I had not been interrupted. "Joe said that the demand for pilots is going to be much greater than the supply. So another program is in the works, a program to train ladies"—I glared at him now—"to fly any old kind of aircraft. Volunteers must be willing to get a pilot's license on their own and then take classes at an army air force base in Texas."

I turned to Liz. "Joe said that you're a natural and that he could take over your training where Mother left off. Think of it, Liz. You could help win the war *and* make your dream come true at the same time. Lessons would be expensive, but you could use some of your inheritance money to pay for them, and you could use Mother's Cub. Joe said that the two of you could work something out. I—"

Uncle Wilbert broke in—again. "She'll never make it! Forget planes. Forget flying." He took a puff on his cigar. "Girls aren't meant to be pilots, especially at her age."

I was ready for this too. "If eighteen-year-old boys can ferry planes, why can't eighteen-year-old girls do the same? After all, they'll get the same instruction, in fact, the best in the whole world, which, because you value education so highly, should please you. Liz," I said as straight-faced as possible, "could go to charm school when the war's over."

Wilbert opened his mouth to say something, then closed it again without uttering a sound. Father bowed his head, and Aunt Tina dabbed at her eyes with a white hanky.

"It's up to you, Liz," I said.

She didn't speak. She didn't have to. For the first time in a year, I saw a smile on her face. As I said before, it was a perfect day, and best of all, it was a new beginning for Liz.

Chapter 3

To my great joy and Uncle Wilbert's consternation, I, Elizabeth Margaret Erickson, soon learned that Joe Sipple's sources were right. In August, government agents began to take applications from women who were at least 18 years old and wanted to ferry planes for the army air force. The program was not without controversy, though. Critics argued that women were too weak and too emotionally fragile to ferry planes. Besides, naysayers asked, what had become of the manhood of America? Couldn't this war be won without the help of women?

Given the country's current mood, a single crash would have caused so much public outrage that the ferrying program would not have been able to continue, so leaders of the program were very fussy about whom they accepted for training. Out of thousands of applicants who wanted to ferry, only a handful were admitted.

Well aware of the fact that the standards were incredibly high, I did everything possible to prepare myself, and Jimmy did all he could to help me. After our little round with Uncle Wilbert at my birthday party, Father, Jimmy, and I decided to fire our cleaning lady. We then divided the chores among the three of us. Jimmy even willingly took on some of my responsibilities, including a little cooking, so that I'd have more time to fly. To cheer me on, he also accompanied me as often as he could when I went to the airfield.

Sipple's airfield was a small-town operation. It had a windsock; a meadow, which a local farmer mowed, for taxiing; a few hangars where the planes were kept; and Joe's office, a messy one-room building. The office windows hadn't been washed since the day they were put in, sometime in the mid-1920s, and the concrete floor was cracked and stained. Out-of-date calendars with photos of pretty movie stars hung from rusty nails all over the walls, and every corner of the room was filled with stacks of yet more calendars and old newspapers. In the middle of the room stood a battered table that served as Joe's desk. It was covered with clipboards chock-full of yellowed sheets of paper and surrounded by four well-worn, mismatched kitchen chairs.

Even though the airfield wasn't the neatest that I had ever seen, it was special to me. I loved the smell that hovered over the place: a combination of motor oil, gasoline, and greasy rags. I also loved the sound of a perfectly tuned engine and the sight of a plane—any plane—against a brilliant blue sky. Even more, I loved the stories that Joe, who had been a pilot in World War I, would tell me whenever there was a lull in business.

Joe is a short, stocky man with thick black hair that juts out in all directions. He always wears an old leather aviator jacket—even in the hottest weather—and well-worn tan slacks that are too long for him. Although Joe has talked endlessly about taking in a partner, he still runs the field by himself, repairing engines, preparing planes for flight, and giving lessons to an increasingly large number of students, for he has quite a reputation as an instructor in this area.

After Mother died, Joe repeatedly offered to give me lessons when I was ready to fly again. For the longest time, I just couldn't climb into a cockpit, but now that I had a goal—at the very least to prove Uncle Wilbert wrong—I was ready to accept Joe's offer. He, in turn, did everything he could to help me. When gas rationing hit hard on the home front, Joe successfully begged other pilots to give their share to me so that I could continue to work toward my license. And he worked with me day or night, trying to make me the perfect pilot.

Joe made me practice my landings until I thought I could put the Cub down in my sleep. "Anyone," Joe said, "can get a plane into the air. Getting it down in one piece is the real trick." I know that I did more touch-and-gos (land, taxi, then take off again) than any of his other students. "Level those wings, Liz," was Joe's favorite line. I wondered how they could get any more level, but I always went through the motions anyway. Eventually my landings, even on sod, were so smooth that Joe could have had a cup of coffee filled to the brim in the cockpit and not have spilled a drop when I touched the ground. Although Joe kept telling me that I had to do better—be it banking the plane or taking off or, his favorite, landing—I saw him smile a lot when he thought I wasn't watching.

By late 1942, I had completed the requirements for my license. When I passed my flight test with high grades, Joe was as happy as I was, and he rightfully took great pride in what I had accomplished.

With license in hand, I wrote to Jacqueline Cochran, who was in charge of the Women's Flying Training Detachment in Texas, for an application form. Mrs. Cochran was a famous aviatrix who had set speed records in the air and had won numerous races in the 1930s, including the world-famous Bendix race. She had approached government officials about using women to ferry planes even before the war began, believing that America would eventually be drawn into the conflict and needed to be as prepared as possible. But officials then didn't believe that women could ferry military planes.

So Cochran and a few female pilots headed to England to make their point. At that time, the English were under a heavy assault by Germany, and they would accept help from anyone, even women pilots. These women, besides ferrying aircraft, repeatedly risked their lives by rushing to planes on the ground during bombing raids to get the surplus aircraft off the ground and out of the reach of the Germans.

When the United States entered the war, Cochran campaigned for a ferrying service under her command, using the women's experience in England as proof of what they could do. After numerous presentations, including one before President and Mrs. Roosevelt, Cochran finally found the support she needed, and the WFTD was formed.

At the same time, army air force leaders asked Nancy Love, also a well-known pilot, to organize a group of highly experienced female pilots for immediate service. Posters were sent to all airports throughout the country to try to recruit pilots. Unlike the women in the WFTD, Love's pilots would not need training, and pilots like me need not apply.

Once I had submitted my application, there was little I could do but wait and hope and pray. Finally, after what seemed like an eternity, I was told to report to Ft. Snelling, an army base in Minneapolis, for a physical exam and an interview. I was more nervous about my upcoming physical than I had been about my flight test. I hadn't had a check-up for more than a year, and as always, I was afraid that my blood tests might indicate that I had diabetes. Diabetics often suffer from vision problems, and worse yet, some can even slip into comas if they can't control the amount of sugar in their blood. Not only would the discovery of the diabetes end any opportunity I might have to enter the ferrying program, the disease would most likely end any hopes I might have of flying.

Jimmy and Father insisted that I had nothing to worry about. To show his support, Father pushed aside piles of unfinished work to take me to my appointment. He even waited patiently for hours on end while doctors examined me, pricking my earlobes and fingertips for blood samples, looking for any and every possible weakness.

Once the testing and questioning were over, I settled down for another long wait. Although I tried hard not to think about being accepted, it was always on my mind, and questions plagued me night and day: Had I answered the questions during my interview to the best of my ability? Did I pass my physical? How do my hours of flight time compare to those of the other applicants? Was Joe's recommendation strong enough? And most important, when, oh, when, would a decision come?

The news that I had so eagerly sought was *finally* delivered by a messenger from Western Union on December 2 at exactly 4:02 P.M. There was great rejoicing in our home as we took turns reading the short, but important, message aloud.

AVIATION CADET EXAMINATION SUCCESSFUL PD PLEASE ADVISE BY RETURN WIRE IF INTERESTED IN POSSIBLE OPENING ONE FEBRUARY FOR TRAINING PD IF SO FURTHER PAPERS WILL BE SENT FOR COMPLETION PD

SIGNED COCHRAN
ARNOLD COMMANDING GENERAL AAF

We held a little party the next evening and invited
friends and relatives to share our joy. Mrs. Smallman
baked several cakes, chocolate this time, which she served
with vanilla ice cream and hot fudge sauce. I was certain
that she had been saving sugar, which was also rationed,
for quite a while to be able to use so much at one time. Joe
gave me a good luck charm, a small gold four-leaf clover,
that he had carried with him all through World War I. I
cried when I opened the box and realized what was inside,
and I saw Father wipe away a tear or two as well. Uncle
Wilbert and Aunt Tina did not join our celebration.

Chapter 4

Early in the morning on January 30, 1943, Father and Jimmy took me to Eau Claire to catch a train to Chicago for the first leg of my two-day journey to Houston. The train station stands at the foot of a hill on the edge of the city's business district. The station's a noisy place when trains arrive and depart; engines hiss and chug along, pulling long lines of passenger cars behind them on one of several tracks leading in and out of the railroad yard. The main building, which is made from blocks of sandstone that have turned dark brown over the years, is marked by a large white sign that bears the city's name.

In addition to the typical travelers, six young men were on their way to enlist in the armed services and family members and sweethearts had come to see them off. These young men were brave and confident, and although most of the women clearly tried to be cheerful, several could not stop crying. All talked loudly and rapidly, which betrayed their nervousness, and from what I could overhear, they chose their words carefully. No one wanted to say the wrong thing or part with a loved one on a bitter note. All of us knew only too well that some of these men would not be coming back alive. My thoughts were interrupted by the conductor's shouting, which forced me to realize that the moment of parting was finally here.

"All aboard! All aboard for Chicago!"

Father and Jimmy hugged me one more time and promised to write. Then, like many others, we tearfully parted on the platform next to the tracks. I quickly boarded the "400," found my seat, and opened my window so that I might say good-bye to Father and Jimmy one more time.

As the train began to pull out of the station, Jimmy raised his hand slightly and gave me his favorite—and best—salute. "Here's looking at you, kid," he said, fighting back tears. "Here's looking at you."

Leaving Father and Jimmy—especially Jimmy!—made me sad. Yet, impossible as it may seem, at the same time I was happy and excited. My heart beat rapidly, and the palms of my hands, despite the cold in my passenger car, were as sweaty as they used to be when I had to give a speech in school. Dramatic scenes raced through my head. I saw myself flying powerful military aircraft, delivering one after another to bases under the most difficult conditions with a skill that amazed every onlooker. I was so happy that, given a little encouragement, I would have sung a song at the top of my lungs, that is, if I could have calmed down long enough to recall the words.

Although it wasn't easy to do, I eventually forced myself to concentrate on the scenery outside my window. Last night's snowfall of big, flat flakes glistened in the sunlight, on occasion making the landscape so bright that I had to squint in order to continue looking.

I had never been south of Chicago before, so from there on, everything was new to me. I was amazed at the flatness of the farmland in central Illinois. It really was, just as one of my geography teachers had said, as level as a tabletop. Within a few hours, barns, silos, and two-story farmhouses had given way to rolling hills and deep river valleys that twisted and turned in the earth. I took it all in, struggling to see long after the sun had set and darkness had blanketed the land.

When I could see little but lights now and then outside my window, I decided to change my view and go to the dining car, which turned out to be a very pleasant room. Crisp, white linen squares covered tables that lined each side of the car. Silverware and water goblets glistened in the soft light, and smiling waiters hustled back and forth in the narrow center aisle to take orders or bring the special of the day. Passengers talked, laughed, and ate slowly, lingering over pots of freshly brewed coffee before leaving the car. In fact, it was nearly nine o'clock when I and the last of the diners departed.

Under normal circumstances, I probably would have

called it a day. But even though my berth in the sleeper car was ready, I knew that I was still too keyed up to rest, so I decided to return to my seat.

Since it was too dark outside to see anything, I studied my fellow travelers. Some, especially those who had boarded recently, had wonderful Southern accents, the first I'd ever heard. I imitated them, trying to replace what is often known as Midwestern twang with something that I thought was more civilized. My feeble attempts were covered by the rhythmic clickety-clack of the wheels as the train moved along the tracks. I continued watching and listening until well past midnight.

When I awoke in the morning, an entirely new scene awaited me. The train had long ago left the snow behind. Now in Mississippi, the train passed through stands of tall evergreens that had the biggest cones I'd ever seen. I'm sure that some would have measured a foot in length and width. At breakfast, a fellow passenger told me that the trees were loblolly pines. By lunchtime, the forests had been replaced with flat cotton fields. Now and then the broad Mississippi River, rusty brown in color and full of silt, came into view.

As soon as the train entered Louisiana, the landscape changed once again. I was astonished by the lush vegetation before me. Ancient oaks, wider than they were tall and draped with long strands of Spanish moss, towered above flowering shrubs. Jasmine vines clung to tree trunks, covered shrubs, and scrambled over old wood fences, while small plants on the ground pushed each other aside as they reached for sunlight. A multitude of meandering streams and vast swamps made it seem as if the state was more water than land. It was a real contrast to Wisconsin, to say the least.

Late that afternoon, I changed trains in New Orleans and finally started to head west. Now that Houston was not far away, I was excited one moment and afraid the next. As I neared my destination, conflicting thoughts raced back and forth in my head. *What a joy it will be to fly every day! What makes you think that you will succeed? I was trained by the best. Yeah. In Chippewa Falls.*

"Houston! Next stop is Houston!" the conductor shouted as he walked through the car.

I rose, straightened my suit jacket, and prepared to meet my fate.

Chapter 5

As I stepped off the train with my suitcase in hand and headed toward the depot's main door, a man in uniform approached me.

"Miss Erickson?"

"Yes?"

"I'm from Hughes Airfield. You look just like the picture on your application," he noted as he slipped my photo into a folder. "You are the last person to arrive today. The others are waiting on the bus that will take us to the airfield and a brief orientation. This way, please."

I followed him to a strange contraption, a truck cab that pulled a large enclosed wagon, which one entered through two big doors in the rear. To be honest, the whole thing looked like the kind of wagon that is often used in Wisconsin to take cattle to the market, except for the fact that this wagon had windows. As I entered the makeshift bus, I noticed long benches on each side. I slipped my suitcase beneath the last opening and sat down. Somehow this wasn't exactly what I'd expected.

The woman next to me turned and smiled. "I'm Mandy Lou Evans," she said in a very distinct Southern drawl, "from Georgia. Welcome aboard."

Mandy Lou was so tiny that I couldn't imagine how she had passed the height test. She had long chestnut-brown hair, brown eyes highlighted with a few specks of gold, an upturned nose, and a slightly crooked smile. Even though we didn't have exclusive stores in Chippewa, I could recognize expensive clothing when I saw it, and it only took me a moment to appraise her beige suit, matching coat, and gold jewelry. Mandy Lou was cute, perky, and far from poor.

"I'm Liz Erickson," I replied, "from Wisconsin. I'm happy to meet you."

I hadn't finished my sentence before I felt the wagon move. We traveled in silence, in large part because it would have been difficult not to do so, since the truck's noisy engine would have drowned out all but the most determined speakers. Sometimes we were lost in our own thoughts; sometimes we stole brief glimpses of the others in the wagon, 20 in all.

After we arrived at Hughes Airfield, which was part of Houston's city airport, we were taken to a classroom, where the base commander and four classmates who had arrived earlier awaited us. We filed in, took our seats, and studied the tall man who stood at the podium. He had perfect posture, an immaculate uniform, and glistening white hair.

When the last woman was seated and the commander had our full attention, he cleared his throat and began. "I'm Major Hogan, the commander of the 319th Army Air Force Flight Training Detachment. Please rise to take your oath of office. Raise your right hand and repeat after me. I, state your name, do solemnly swear. . . ."

After completing the oath, which made us eligible for training, Major Hogan explained the program to us. "We do not have proper facilities for ladies on this base," he said. "Therefore, you will be billeted in Houston. You will be bused here each day until the entire operation can be moved to Avenger Field, in Sweetwater, Texas, which is currently being used to train pilots for the British Air Force.

"Your day will be divided into four parts. Since ferrying planes requires strength and endurance, you'll begin with a vigorous exercise program each morning. Half of you will have ground school after your workout, while the other half is in the air. In the afternoon, you'll reverse positions. In the evening, you'll study. Although the program is part of the army air force, we have contracted with Aviation Enterprises to provide the necessary instructors, and you will take orders from them. All of your final tests, however, will be conducted by army air force personnel.

"Ground school," he continued, "will hold classes six

days a week. This is only our third group, and we are still refining our program. Right now, we believe that it will take twenty-two to twenty-three weeks to train you. You will take courses in meteorology, engines, instrumentation, navigation, aircraft design, physics, mathematics, and communications. If you complete the course, you will have approximately two hundred hours of ground school training, perhaps more."

I took a deep breath and let it out slowly. I had expected to take some classes, but not 200 hours' worth.

"You will begin flight lessons in the PTs, primary trainers," he added. "The planes for advanced training are now tied up with the classes ahead of you. If—if—you pass your PT flight test, you will go on to BTs—basic trainers—as soon as they are available, and finally ATs—advanced trainers with twin engines. If you pass the AT test, you will become a ferry pilot at one of four bases: Dallas, Texas; Long Beach, California; Romulus, Michigan; or New Castle, Delaware."

He glanced at his notes before continuing. "As you know, our enemies are determined, powerful, and extremely well supplied. They have also been, to date, very successful. The Germans now occupy the Rhineland, Poland, Austria, Czechoslovakia, Norway, Denmark, the Netherlands, Belgium, Luxembourg, and France. Currently they are attacking the Soviet Union and England, which they expect to defeat soon. The Italians have laid claim to Albania, Ethiopia, Egypt, and Greece. The Japanese have invaded Manchuria, China, Thailand,

British Malaya, Guam, Hong Kong, the Philippines, Midway Island, Bataan, and Corregidor, most of which they now control.

"As a result, America has a real fight on its hands, and our men and our allies need every plane that they can get to help beat back and then conquer these ruthless invaders. Assembly lines working twenty-four hours a day will soon be able to produce at least sixty thousand planes a year. While this is an incredible accomplishment, I must remind you that these planes are useless to us until they reach our bases. We have many men who can ferry. We'd prefer to have them man bombers at the front, where they are desperately needed, but we can't do that until you can take their ferrying positions." He paused, looking in turn at each of us. "I can't stress this enough. Your country needs you more than you can possibly imagine."

There was a slight rustle in the room. It may have been my imagination, but I thought that several women in front of me suddenly sat up a little straighter than before. Mandy Lou was grinning.

"Your credentials," Major Hogan continued, "are outstanding. With one exception, all of you are college graduates. In addition, most of you have held a pilot's license for several years and have accumulated more than five hundred hours of flight time as well. Some of you have even been flight instructors. As a result, you may think that you are hotshots. Maybe you are, maybe you're not. The point is that although your services are desperately needed, you will be under the army's jurisdiction, and you will fly according to army air force rules and methods, not your own, to prepare to ferry for us. Half—half!—of our previous students couldn't get that through their heads, so we sent them packing."

He let that message sink in before finishing his presentation. "The bus will take you back to Houston now. You will be picked up each day at seven forty-five and delivered at twenty-one hundred—nine P.M. civilian time—until we move the program."

A sense of uneasiness hung over us as we rode back to Houston, where we eventually arrived at Oleander Court, a rundown tourist accommodation. The driver divided us into pairs, using the alphabet to assign roommates. Eventually, Erickson and Evans were taken to room 3.

As we entered our room, Mandy Lou took one look at the furnishings and gasped. "This is awful, just awful!" She ran a finger across a rickety end table beside an old sofa. "Why, this room is shabby and dirty. If my mother saw this, she'd just faint away, and I do mean faint away." Mandy Lou wrinkled her nose as she sniffed the stale air, then proceeded to open a window. Finally, she lifted the corner of a well-worn chenille bedspread and bent down to peek at the floor. She shuddered as several insects scurried for cover. "Oh, no! I think we have cockroaches!"

At this point, I didn't really care if the room had rats. I was exhausted and more than a little worried. I fell upon one of the beds and stared at the ceiling. I was the youngest student in the class and the only one who didn't have a college education. The ferrying program suddenly seemed awfully difficult, and the commander was willing, maybe even eager, to fail us. *What on earth*, I thought, *have I gotten myself into?* As I drifted off to sleep, I saw Wilbert's smiling face.

Chapter 6

$\mathcal{S}$ince women were not part of the armed services, the army air force did not have uniforms for us. Instead, following Cochran's directions, we provided our own outfits. We brought comfortable clothing for physical training, and white blouses and khaki-colored slacks for ground school. We were told that the army would provide us with coveralls for our flight lessons.

As we boarded the bus the next morning, dressed for our exercise class, I was amazed at the variety of clothing I saw: shorts; old gym uniforms; jeans, which ladies never wore in public; and well-worn sweaters and blouses. We were, to be very honest, a motley crew.

Our appearance may not have been the best, but our attitude had improved overnight. I saw a look of determination in my classmates' eyes that was contagious. During the ride to the field, we took turns introducing ourselves and discussing—in detail—what we had found in our rooms at Oleander Court, shouting over the noisy engine in order to be heard. As we exchanged information, we joked about what we might find next.

So we were in good spirits when we were met at the field by our physical education instructor. Dressed in navy shorts and a white T-shirt and apparently eager to begin our classes, he swung open the bus doors and greeted us in a booming voice. "Good morning, ladies! I'm Bob Hanks, the man who's going to get you in shape. Because you're being trained the army way, you'll march to the exercise field in a straight line. In fact, from now on, you'll march to every class, meal, and flight lesson with your chins up and your shoulders back. You'll also march in alphabetical order." As he called off our names, we scrambled to take our places.

I was amazed at how eagerly our group participated in the drills. I remembered only too well that exercises in gym class had been greeted with groans and complaints. But there were no objections today. When our instructor told us to do jumping jacks and knee bends, we did them, even though some of us had to strain. Enthusiasm did wane by the end of the hour as we tried to finish the workout with 20 push-ups, which I just couldn't do.

Mandy Lou couldn't do them either. Between huffs and puffs, she said, "We don't have to worry about being sent packing anymore. Hanks will kill us with push-ups before that happens." My thoughts exactly.

After our workout, we headed to the airport's main

building. We changed into our ground school clothes, ate a hearty breakfast, then divided alphabetically into two groups.

The first group had ground school in the morning. I joined 11 other women in a class about navigation that was scheduled to last until noon. Mandy Lou, Nila Fellenz, and I shared a long table. A tall, thin brunette with gray eyes, Nila was a former high school history teacher from Delaware. She had notebooks and folders, all clearly labeled, which she arranged in neat stacks on the table; newly sharpened pencils; a dictionary; and an atlas. (In contrast, I had an old loose-leaf notebook and two stubby pencils.) She also had a maturity and an aloofness that set her apart from the others. I had to force myself to call her Nila rather than Miss Fellenz.

Our instructor began the session by passing out maps. He had circled specific landforms within several hundred miles and underlined the names of cities and towns that displayed their names on water towers. We would have instrument training later, but until then, we had to use these markers to find our way. We were also expected to expand as quickly as possible our overall knowledge of American geography for cross-country flights. "You never know," our instructor said, "when your instruments might fail. It's best to be prepared for the worst possible situation. Landforms are a dependable way to navigate, and they are the best backup system that we have."

I hadn't worked too hard in my geography classes in high school, and I honestly couldn't identify even a small percentage of the mountain ranges, rivers, or cities in the United States. My argument was that I could always look up whatever I needed if and when I needed it. Although we would carry maps when we ferried, if we overshot our map, or worse yet, lost it—maps had been known to fly out of open-cockpit planes—we would have to rely on our basic knowledge of geography to navigate. Clearly I had some catching up to do.

After lunch, we marched to a supply room, where we received our official flight suits, a man's pair of coveralls, size 44, the smallest that they had. Mandy Lou was the first to don her suit, and she shrieked with laughter when she closed the last snap. Her pants legs dragged on the floor, and her sleeves completely covered her hands. "How," she asked as she paraded about like a clown, "can I fly anything while wearing this?"

The rest of us followed suit—even Nila—laughing at our outfits, comparing coveralls, trying to figure out who looked the worst. When we decided that tiny Mandy Lou had won first place, we set out to make a bad situation better. We rolled up the legs and sleeves and tied belts around our waists as tightly as possible. There was nothing that we could do about the seats, so we just let them swing and sway as we moved about.

Our official uniforms also included goggles to prevent our eyes from watering when we flew in open cockpits, and white scarves. Because most of us had long hair and because flight instructors, who usually sat behind their students in the planes, were afraid that hair blowing in the wind would limit their vision, we were told that the scarves were to be worn as turbans. As I tied mine in place and tested my goggles, I wondered what the instructors at the Mitchell Charm School would think of my outfit.

Each of us was assigned to a flight instructor. Mine was John Jacob. He was a small man with wispy brown hair, soft spoken, and shy. As he began to explain what we were going to do and how we were going to do it, I knew that he knew exactly what he was talking about.

"You'll begin your PT training in a Stearman," he said. "It's an old plane, open cockpit and all, but it's serviceable." He sighed. "It's all the government was willing to give us for the first classes. New PTs are on order, but they won't arrive in time for your lessons." He paused, looking closely at a list of instructions. "Today, you'll simply get acquainted with the plane. We'll go over the checklists, take a short flight so that you can get a feel for this particular aircraft, and talk about safety procedures."

He looked me over. "You're not very tall, but I don't think that you'll need cushions. I'll take one along just in case, though. Some of the girls in the first class were so short that they had to sit on several in order to see out of the cockpit. The record was four."

He picked up a parachute from a stack in the corner of his ready room. "Please put this on."

I took the pack, and he watched carefully as I slipped my arms and legs through straps and then fastened them in front. Convinced that I knew how to put on a parachute, he moved on.

"I assume," he said, "that you know the best way to parachute to safety."

"You climb onto the wing, slide off, count, and pull the cord."

He shook his head. "Too many people have been injured that way, hitting the edge of a wing on some planes or bumping themselves on the edge of the cockpit in their eagerness to get out. It's much better to turn the plane upside down if you can, release your safety belt, fall from the plane, count, then open the chute. Have you ever flown upside down?"

Now I shook my head.

"I'll show you how to turn the plane over today." He scanned a clipboard that he carried, nodding his head slightly. "Let's go to the aircraft."

The Stearman he led me to was about 20 feet long, and I guessed that the wingspan was about 30 feet, maybe 35. It was about the same size as Mother's Cub, and for a moment, I visualized her standing before the craft. I wondered how she, a very cautious pilot, would have reacted to it. Would she have been eager to fly something so much more powerful than her Cub, or would she have resisted the temptation? No question about it. Although the PT was old, I guessed that it might easily reach 100 miles per hour, and I itched to get in, fire it up, and take off.

Instead, we spent more time on the ground. "You begin here," Mr. Jacob said as he walked toward the plane's wheels. "Most of my students have flown planes that were maintained and examined by someone else. You will be responsible for the final check for every plane you fly for us. Never take off before you have checked the tires for cuts, wear, and proper inflation. Check even if the tires were perfect yesterday or even if the plane just rolled off the assembly line.

"Next, examine the wings. Make sure that they are free of mud or snow or ice or anything else, for that matter. What you find will vary from one site to another. Once a pilot found snakes sunning themselves on a wing. They wouldn't cause any trouble in the air, but I'd still leave them on the ground.

"Also, always make sure that the propeller doesn't have a single dent or nick. Take your time and look at every inch."

We walked around the plane as he continued a lengthy preflight checklist—the condition of the gas tanks, oil levels, and much more. I was expected to memorize the list and to follow it faithfully. Failure to do so even once meant being ousted from the program. Period.

When he had finished giving me my checklist, he paused for a moment, as if trying to decide if he should add something. "Check everything, Elizabeth, once, twice, three times if necessary."

I was about to ask him why I should be so cautious, when he suddenly turned away. Afraid to pursue the matter, I stifled my curiosity, at least for the moment.

After removing the chocks—blocks of wood placed by the plane's wheels to prevent rolling—I climbed onto one of the wings and then into the front seat, where I fastened my safety belt. I grinned as I looked around, touching dials, familiarizing myself with the cockpit before Mr. Jacob explained the next checklist that he would use just before taking off. The army's procedure wasn't all that different from the method that Joe had used.

When Mr. Jacob thought that I had the list down pat, he entered the trainer's seat, which had a full set of controls; started the engine; and waited for permission to take off. Through headsets that we wore so that we could communicate with each other in the air, he explained that we would be told to fly in one of the field's quadrants at an altitude of 5,000, 6,000, or 7,000 feet. Dividing the airspace into four sections with three levels each made it possible for 12 students to practice at the same time. However, with a dozen planes in the air, we had to be very careful. We couldn't vary our flight pattern without warning the control tower. "Doing something unexpected," Mr. Jacob said, "could be deadly."

Within minutes Mr. Jacob was taxiing into position. He then increased the engine's revolutions per minute and started down the runway, picking up speed. I felt the plane vibrate as we raced along, and when we began to gain altitude I felt a familiar lurch in my stomach. This was wonderful!

"Elizabeth," Mr. Jacob said, "When you take off and especially when you land, you must look over your shoulder at the horizon to make sure that the plane is level. Aircraft designs vary, and on some models to be ferried, propellers get in the way of a forward view. A rear view is a necessity. Remember that."

I nodded. Believe me, after even a few lessons from Joe, I knew that rule cold.

After climbing to 6,000 feet, we leveled off. "I'll turn the plane upside down now," he said. "This is what you would do to bail out in an emergency if you can still control the plane." He then gently rolled the Stearman over.

I felt blood rush to my head and the pressure inside my skull increase to such a point that I was very uncomfortable. Although I told myself that this wasn't all that different from standing on my head or hanging upside down on a trapeze on a playground, which I had done often as a child, I wasn't sure how long I could endure being upside down in an open cockpit thousands of feet above the ground. But as my safety belt strained to hold me in place, I realized how easy it would be to release the buckle and fall out. This knowledge gave me a sense of security. Even so, I was relieved when Mr. Jacob righted the plane.

"Do you understand how I did that?" he asked.

"Yes."

"Good. Tomorrow I expect you to show me how it's done. You must remember, though, that you can fly upside down only for a short period of time. Doing so interrupts the gas flow to the engine. At the first sound of sputtering you must either fall out or right the plane."

We had flown in a pattern, one plane above us, another below, for less than 10 minutes when Mr. Jacob asked for and received permission to touch down. "Takeoffs and landings are the most dangerous part of flying, Elizabeth, so we practice them often under a variety of conditions. Today we'll do ideal takeoffs and landings, flying into the wind for uplift and then adjusting the flaps and using the wind to slow us down when we land. Eventually we'll deal with strong crosswinds and short landing fields, which you might encounter if you have to make an emergency landing. I'll touch down, taxi, then begin to ascend. I want you to take over as soon as the plane is off the ground. I want to see what you can do. All right?"

"Yes, sir!" I shouted, without even trying to hide my enthusiasm. I patted Joe's lucky charm and a locket containing Mother's picture, both of which now hung around my neck on a long gold chain, and waited for my big moment.

Mr. Jacob's touchdown was so perfect that I was hardly aware that the wheels had hit the runway. He scooted along for a short distance, then began to climb. As soon as he did so, I took the controls, looking over my shoulder at the horizon to keep the wings level. When I reached 6,000 feet, I stopped climbing and flew the pattern that Mr. Jacob had flown.

"Now do a touch-and-go, Elizabeth. Then climb to exactly six thousand feet and turn the controls over to me. I'll bring the craft in."

I followed his directions. My touchdown was rough compared to his and when I climbed for the second time,

I didn't get the plane perfectly level. Still, I thought that I did as well as could be expected for the first day.

We landed without incident. He showed me how to "S" the army way, that is, taxi in an *S* pattern so that I could see what was ahead of me on the runway for a while if the propeller was in the way.

When I climbed out of the plane, Mr. Jacob studied me for a moment, then smiled. "You know, I've had students, highly experienced students, panic on the first day, especially when I showed them how to fall out. That, besides being a safety measure, was a little test. Anyone who has trouble with it usually has trouble with stalls and spins as well, and I like to know that ahead of time. You didn't say a word when I turned the plane over, nor did you show any signs of fear. You're very young. Still . . ." He paused, then offered his hand. "I'm looking forward to working with you."

At the end of the day's lessons and a long study session, we boarded the bus for Houston. Buoyed by our experiences in the air—and almost all of us had had a good day—we were more confident than ever that all of us would succeed. We were not eager to shout over the engine again, so we decided to sing to pass the time. All of us knew the most popular tunes of the day, the majority of which came from movies. When we ran out of show tunes, one of my classmates, who had gotten hold of some lyrics that a girl in a previous class had written, taught us a new song. It was sung to the tune of "Yankee Doodle Dandy."

We are Yankee Doodle pilots,
Yankee Doodle, do or die!
Real live nieces of our Uncle Sam,
Born with a yearning to fly.
Keep in step to all our classes.
March to flight line with our pals.
Yankee Doodle came to Texas
Just to fly the PTs!
We are those Yankee Doodle gals!

I was still humming the tune when we arrived at Oleander Court. Mandy Lou immediately began to organize her books and papers for yet another study session, and I decided to join her. If I had to memorize every landform in the United States, I would do so. If I had to fly upside down and even fall out, I would do that too. I was—and I was determined to remain—a Yankee Doodle gal.

Chapter 7

During the next two weeks, my flight lessons went very well. Mr. Jacob was a good teacher, and he clearly loved what he was doing. Actually, at times it was hard to know who enjoyed the lessons more, the teacher or the student.

On several occasions, we finished my assignment early. Since neither of us wanted to lose a minute of flight time that had been allotted to us, I used the extra time to practice, while Mr. Jacob rode along. But one especially bright, sunny day when cumulus clouds were popping up here and there, he took the controls. We flew off base, gliding over, under, between, and around the billowing forms. It was a flawless ride, smooth and seemingly effortless as he banked left, then right, gently rising and falling as we met the puffy stuff. I wanted the ride to last forever.

But although my lessons in the air were going well, no

matter how hard I worked, ground school proved to be very difficult. Unlike my college-educated classmates, I had a lot to learn. Not only were they better informed in geography, math, and science, they seemed to have learned so much outside the classroom. Most of them even knew the Morse Code, which was now part of our communications class. They had been Girl Scouts when they were younger, and they had memorized all the dots and dashes then. Mandy Lou said that every girl in Savannah had been a scout—after all, the group's founder, Juliette Low, had lived in Savannah. I thought that "every girl" was an exaggeration, but I didn't say so.

What surprised me the most was that even if my classmates didn't know anything about a particular subject, they seemed to learn the material faster than I did and with a lot less work. This, I eventually figured out, was due to the fact that they had good study skills, something else I hadn't bothered to learn in school.

When I found myself falling further and further behind and I was certain that I was about to fail, I swallowed my pride and turned to Nila for help. I thought that she might give me a lecture—as teachers sometimes do—about not learning when I had had the opportunity. I was prepared to endure this if it meant that she would give me some help. But instead of treating me like a delinquent student, she regarded me as an adult who was eager to learn. She said something about the privilege of teaching a willing pupil, then spent several hours going over the next day's lessons, showing me how she would study for them. I learned how to read more accurately, select key items, take notes, and review material. This made studying easier. Even so, I still had to work late into the night and spend my day off curled up with my assignments.

If there was any spare time, we used it to try to get the latest news. Mandy Lou bought a radio so that we could listen to an evening broadcast once in a while, and whenever possible, I bought a newspaper at the airfield. As could be expected, the headlines were mostly about the war. In mid-February, the Japanese had finally been stopped at Guadalcanal in the South Pacific, but German and Italian forces were gaining ground in North Africa. The best news we could find concerned the Russian front. Although the Germans who invaded Russia had thought that they could easily beat the Soviets, the Russians had drawn the line deep in Soviet territory at Stalingrad. There the Russians fought valiantly. The invaders, who were far from home or any creature comforts, were suffering the effects of a particularly brutal winter and, as a result, they were demoralized and in great disarray.

Even though America and its allies were beginning to beat back their enemies, the war was far from over. We had land to recover on three continents, and winning a battle one day didn't necessarily mean that we would do the same the following morning. Our enemies were not quitters.

So fear of invasion was still widespread on our coasts. Volunteers watched the sky at night for signs of enemy bombers. In large cities—which government officials believed would be the enemies' main targets if an attack took place—people established emergency shelters, complete with food and water. Because American officials thought that the Germans or Japanese might use poisonous gases during an invasion, gas masks were issued to people in these cities as well. To become familiar with the masks, everyone was encouraged to wear them whenever possible, working in the yard, for example, which was quite a sight when a whole neighborhood donned its headgear at the same time. Men too old to enlist and some young women began to take weapons classes so that they could defend their communities if the enemy landed. Others learned how to drive ambulances or provide emergency medical care.

In addition, everyone was told to refrain from giving out any information to strangers. We were certain that spies were at work everywhere, and even a little bit of information in a letter from the front or something overheard at work might prove useful to our enemies. Signs with pictures of sinking ships and slogans such as "Someone Talked" hung in most public buildings.

One of the groups thought to be spying and potentially sympathetic to Japan were the Japanese-Americans. The government placed them in internment camps, where they were expected to remain throughout the war. This action was not without controversy.

At the same time that Americans were learning how to protect the home front, they were trying to find more and more ways to support the war effort. These good citizens included some students in Chippewa, according to Jimmy's latest letter.

February 15, 1943

Dear Liz,

I have so much to tell you!

Father got tired of my cooking, so he hired Mrs. Smallman to prepare meals for us three nights a week. Father told her to make big roasts (if she can get the meat) or big pots of soup so that we would have lots of leftovers to eat on the other days. She's actually thinking about starting a catering business, and because there are so many working wives now, she could do well. Father told her to give it a try, and he even offered to loan her some money to get started if she needed it.

Bigger event, yet! I've been asked to write a skit for an all-school presentation. The Junior High Volunteers Club has decided to do more for the war effort. Besides the scrap metal and paper drives, we're going to encourage kids to help with the food drive. They can either plant victory gardens this summer or help local farmers plant and harvest crops. Farmers around here are really shorthanded now, since everyone's at Smith's. That's where I come in. I'm going to write a skit that will get kids to join up. The only problem is that the club has been given a new advisor, Miss Preston! Ugh! She told me right away that she didn't want my skit to be too dramatic, whatever that means.

Father said that I could have a V garden. I'm going to plant carrots, tomatoes, onions, and maybe potatoes in the open spot in the backyard by the rhubarb patch. Father wants rutabagas too, but I won't plant them. I can't stand those bitter things

I visited Joe at the airfield yesterday. All is going well there, although with gas rationing now, he isn't able to give many lessons. Joe asks about you all the time. I can't tell him anything if you don't write. So write to me!

Father sends his love.

Love,
Jim

P.S. For whatever reason, Uncle Wilbert hasn't visited us since you left. Hurrah!!!

Hurrah, indeed.

Chapter 8

Although all of my classmates were equally determined to succeed, some of us were experiencing serious problems by the end of February. While I continued to struggle with ground school, others worked hard to learn how to pull planes out of stalls and spins, both of which were difficult and frightening.

In order to get a plane to stall, we'd climb straight up until the plane's wings couldn't get enough lift to support the aircraft. We then dropped toward the earth, nose first. During the rapid descent, we had to learn how to keep the plane from twisting and turning until we could level it off. Although no one would deliberately stall a plane being ferried, or any plane other than a trainer for that matter, stalls could occur anytime someone started to climb too rapidly. This exercise was simply a safety precaution.

So was learning how to pull out of spins. To make a

plane spin, we would pull the control stick way back, then
apply full rudder either left or right, depending upon
which way the plane was supposed to turn. I did not look
forward to twisting in the air while dropping toward the
earth in an open cockpit. It was only by willing myself to
keep calm and putting all of my trust in Mr. Jacob's
methods of stopping the spin—again using the control
stick and rudders—that I managed to function at all.

The hardest part during both stalls and spins was
remembering not to pull up too fast. It was only natural to
want to get the nose of the plane up into the air as quickly
as possible, but doing so could cause the plane to stall,
putting it into a dive again. Only this time there would be
less space between the plane and the ground.

By the end of the fourth week, four classmates had, in
the words of Major Hogan, "been sent packing." Spins
understandably sent them into a panic, and they couldn't
pull their Stearmans out of danger without help. As the
women bid us farewell, we looked about and wondered
aloud who would be next.

During the day, we ventured farther and farther from
the field, using landmarks and water towers to guide us.
We also began to fly our planes at night in anticipation of
our cross-country flights. Although I couldn't wait for
night flight instruction, Mandy Lou fought it. "I can't see
any sense in it," she argued. "Why can't we just ferry in
the daylight? It would be so much safer. At least I could
see the landmarks. Why should we add risk to our flights
when we don't have to?"

I told her how beautiful the sky was at night, but I couldn't convince her.

With our instructor's permission, we could practice on our own when classes were over. I eagerly sought the extra hours, for my PT check test was rapidly approaching. On March 2, I went to the flight line, selected a plane, and asked for and received permission to take off. I climbed to 5,000 feet in my quadrant. I knew that I should practice recovering from stalls, so I started to climb. I hadn't gone far when my plane began to drop. I struggled to keep the Stearman from spinning, pulling out as well as could be expected. As I looked over my shoulder to make sure that I had leveled off properly, I took a little extra time to enjoy the sights. When I looked forward again, I could hardly believe my eyes. My engine was on fire!

Neither Joe nor Mr. Jacob had prepared me for this. I didn't know if I should try to bring the PT in or turn it over and bail out. I started to turn, then changed my mind. I thought about calling the tower to request permission to land, then thought that the fire, which was spreading rapidly, was too far along to make that possible. So I thought about bailing out again. "Make up your mind!" I shouted to no one but myself. "Jump or land! It's that simple!" After a few more moments of weighing the odds, I finally decided to land.

In as calm a voice as I could manage, I radioed the tower and told the flight controller about the fire. I could hear a lot of commotion in the background and a man yelling "Clear the runway! Now! Get everyone out of her quadrant!" Obviously someone on the ground had already spotted the smoke and flames and preparations were under way for an emergency landing. I wondered aloud what they thought my chances were of reaching the runway in one piece.

As I began to descend as rapidly as I could, I tried to ignore the flames and to concentrate on the landing strip. This, of course, proved to be more difficult than I thought it would be. The blaze was spreading, reaching back toward me, getting closer every second.

Suddenly I felt sick. Muscles in my neck and back became taut, and I could sense the beginning of powerful and painful spasms. My stomach was anything but settled, and my heart was racing. My hands were so sweaty that I could barely keep a grip on the control stick. For the first time in my life, I could feel fear—real fear—starting to take hold of me. I wondered if this was what my mother had felt when she and Wilbert had plunged to the earth.

I also wondered how much longer I could keep my emotions under control.

My nerves were raw, and I felt like screaming one second and crying the next.

I struggled to keep the plane as level as possible as I dropped in altitude, even though I just wanted to point the nose straight down and take my chances. I was circling down now, less than 4,000 feet above the runway. I took a deep breath, then another to try to calm myself.

Three thousand feet. Another deep breath. Black smoke now poured from the engine, making it nearly impossible for me to see in front of the plane.

Now tears were rolling down my cheeks and my whole body was shaking. I did not want to die today, especially not in a plane crash, but if I couldn't control myself, that was exactly what was going to happen. I continued to try to hold on and to descend.

One thousand feet. Now I not only worried about flames and smoke, I wondered how much longer my engine would continue to function. I gripped the control stick with one hand and knowing that I would have but one chance to line up the Stearman with the runway, wiped the tears from my eyes, trying to improve my vision.

Five hundred feet.

Four hundred.

Three.

Two.

The runway! I could feel the runway!

My landing was the worst that I had ever made, a series of rough bounces that would have thrown me from the plane if I hadn't been wearing my safety belt. As soon as I brought the Stearman to a stop, I jumped out of the cockpit. I thought about running from the field just to get away from this nightmare, but my wobbly legs wouldn't have carried me far.

By this time mechanics in the hangars, instructors, and several students waiting to take off, including Nila, had gathered round to help. The mechanics smothered the fire with a white foam while Nila tried to calm me down. I'm not sure which was harder to do.

When the fire was completely out and the mechanics and instructors had left the scene, Nila insisted upon checking my plane. While I stood to the side, she poked about, eventually pulling out some charred remnants of fabric from the engine. "From now on," she said sternly, "check your engine for old rags."

I just stared at her.

"I repeat," she said in a tone I think that she must have used often as a teacher, "check your engine from now on. And while you're at it, check for anything else that's out of place. In the meantime, say nothing about this to anyone. I'll tell the other women to check their planes."

"A mechanic must have left the rag there by accident, Nila. Surely you don't think that . . ."

"My fuel and oil lines were hooked up improperly yesterday. It's impossible for any mechanic to have made such a mistake. Two questionable events are two events too many."

"But why . . . ?" The grim look on Nila's face and her suspicions so stunned me that I couldn't continue. I simply stumbled back to the barracks.

Instead of studying that evening, I lay on my bed and stared at the ceiling. A few minutes later, Mandy Lou put her lessons aside and turned toward me. "Liz," she said softly. "What's wrong?"

I remained silent for a few moments. "One minute I'm afraid to climb back into a cockpit," I said. "That makes me feel like a coward, and I hate that. The next minute I want to rush to the flight line and take up every PT on the

60

airfield to announce to the weasel who tampered with my plane—if there is a weasel—that I won't be scared off."

"I can understand why you were afraid," Mandy Lou replied. "Anyone with any sense would have been scared silly. But you're not the only one who has ever been frightened, Liz. We've all been afraid in the air. You have to put this behind you. Fear will make you too tense to fly well, and being angry may lead to some poor decision-making. Please don't let this awful fire ruin your chances of becoming a ferry pilot."

How often have I been warned about how my emotions might affect my flying? I asked myself. *At least a hundred times by Mother, who insisted that no one should fly when upset, and at least a dozen times more by Joe.*

When I didn't respond, Mandy Lou continued. "I honestly can't believe that someone is out to hurt us," Mandy Lou said. "But if Nila's suspicions are right, we should be able to scare off whoever is doing this by checking our planes and making a point of watching everyone's actions in the hangars."

"Maybe."

"So report to the flight line tomorrow as scheduled. And just take up one plane. All right?"

I did as she said. Within a week, I felt comfortable again—comfortable, but not completely safe. I was constantly looking over my shoulder now, and it wasn't always to make sure that the wings of my plane were level.

Chapter 9

On March 10, my class moved to Avenger Field, in Sweetwater, which is located near Abilene, about 300 miles northwest of Houston. Avenger, devoted entirely to training women, was the first base of its kind in American history.

My class arrived in style, ferrying all the PTs to the field, including some new planes, which had been delivered to us only days before. As we neared the airfield, we formed a long line in the sky. As I looked at the area below, I was amazed at the number of cars I could see lining the roads leading to the airport. I was flattered that so many people would take an interest in our program and come out to welcome us. One after another we requested permission to land, and after doing so, watched as our classmates flew in. When the last plane had landed, we marched to our new living quarters.

We were assigned to military barracks, which were a great improvement over Oleander Court, even if the barracks were sparse, to say the least. Because Ann Albert, who was the first to be tested in a PT, had failed her check flight, our class now had 19 students. Nine of us were housed in the first section; the other 10 were billeted next door. Each section had a bathroom and two bedrooms, each of which contained six military cots and six metal lockers. That was it—no curtains, no rugs, no chairs, and no pretty pictures on the walls. I shared a room with Mandy Lou, Nila, and Barbara Cox, the only redhead (and the only person who had a million freckles and green eyes) in our class. Barbara, a former airline stewardess, was from Oregon and, like me, had gotten her pilot's license just before being accepted for the ferrying program. She was outgoing and cheerful and not above pulling a prank or two.

After settling in, we were told that we were subject to inspection every Saturday morning. This meant that from now on our beds had to be made the army way. Besides making what are known as "hospital corners," bed linens had to be so taut that a quarter would bounce when dropped on the top blanket.

In addition, everything had to be spotless. An official wearing white gloves would check our floors, the tops of the lockers, the windows, even the light bulbs. If his gloves picked up as much as a speck of dust, everyone in the room would be denied the privilege of leaving the airfield later that afternoon. Not only that, if we accumulated enough demerits for sloppy housekeeping, we could be sent home.

So we practiced making beds. Nila didn't complain, but Mandy Lou wasn't real happy about the rules. "Who cares," she muttered, "if a quarter bounces? I can sleep real well on a bed that's not stretched tight as a trampoline."

"Just do it," Barbara replied. "I'm going to go around and drop quarters on all the beds in the room. I love to jitterbug, and if there's a dance within fifty miles of here on a Saturday night, I'll find it. Remember, I have a car, and if we pass inspection, I'll take you with me. If we don't pass, I'll be crabby and impossible to live with all weekend. It's your choice."

I laughed. I couldn't imagine that Barbara would ever be crabby. But when she went around checking beds, I knew that she was serious. Barbara dropped a quarter on Mandy Lou's bed three times, and when the coin just lay there, Barbara turned to Mandy Lou, raising her eyebrows in warning. "Get it right by inspection time," she said matter-of-factly.

Saturday morning, two hours before our inspector was to arrive, Barbara checked our progress. When we met her standards, after two bed remakes on Mandy Lou's part, we were certain that we could pass any inspector's eagle eye. Our biggest problem, besides taut sheets and blankets, was trying to remove every grain of grit from our room. Avenger Airfield was surrounded by sand, which worked its way through slits around the doors and even through window screens with the help of the never-ending winds.

So we mopped floors, washed windowsills, and dusted every surface in the room. It was a lot of work. And it was worth it, for we passed our inspection with little difficulty.

That afternoon, we put on our best outfits. It had been more than a month since we had worn pretty dresses, silk stockings, high heels, and makeup, and it was a welcome change.

When everyone was ready, we piled into Barbara's car to go to Sweetwater. As we rode along, we were amazed at the vastness of the landscape. All of us had heard about being able to see forever, but we hadn't believed it until now. Unlike Wisconsin, where hills or forests often interrupted my view of the rural horizon, in Texas I could see for miles and miles. We took turns guessing how far away something was, making mental notes to check out each site when we had an opportunity to do so.

We quickly discovered that Sweetwater was an interesting little town that could have served as a set for a Western movie. Even though it was 1943, men still wore cowboy boots, spurs, and ten-gallon hats, which they tipped when meeting ladies on the streets. The smell of sagebrush dominated the air, and the sight of the wide-open spaces was never far away. The Blue Bonnet Hotel, which had a drugstore and a soda fountain where we could get a Coke for a nickel, was the main building in town. The hotel was surrounded by wood buildings that had been weathered by wind and sand. "I thought that this only existed in the movies," Mandy Lou whispered. "I expect to see a posse riding into town any minute."

We splurged on supper at the hotel. As we entered the dining room, all of the other diners became silent and watched us closely as we crossed the room and took our seats.

"Why are they looking at us?" I asked.

"This is a small town," Nila replied. "They know we're strangers. They've also probably guessed that we're part of the ferrying program, which makes us even more interesting."

"Are they friendly or hostile?" Barbara asked. "I can't tell."

"I'll bet they're in awe of us," I replied. "Remember how many came out just to see us arrive when we moved to Sweetwater?"

Nila smiled. "Is that what you think? That they came to greet us? I have it on very good authority that most of the people who came to the field that day came to see if we'd really be able to land our planes. Some actually made bets about how many crashes there would be."

"I don't believe it!" Barbara shouted. She looked around the room. "Of all the insults!"

Nila laughed. "Remember, our program is the first of its kind. You can't really blame people for being a little skeptical."

"Skeptical is one thing," Barbara said, "betting that I'll crash is another. Well, I hope they all lost a lot of money!"

Although we hadn't planned to talk shop, shortly after our soup arrived our conversation turned to our upcoming PT tests. Until Ann Albert had failed, most of us had thought that the tests would be little more than routine. After all, our instructors seemed to be very pleased with our progress, and we were absolutely certain that we were better than the two classes before us. But after Ann's failure, we had become apprehensive.

"I hate to say it," Nila said, "but I think that the check pilots will fail a certain number of us no matter how good we are."

"Why?" I asked. "Major Hogan told us how badly our services are needed. It doesn't make any sense to just get rid of us."

Nila leaned forward and spoke softly so that we were the only ones in the room who could hear her. "First of all, the army has to prove that the program's standards are very high. To do that, officials simply can't pass every student, even if each and every one of us is perfect. So some are going to fail no matter what.

"Second, not everyone wants us to succeed. Although army air force leaders want the program to fly, some military men, and some members of the public, believe that women should be home cooking and cleaning, not ferrying planes. If we get a check pilot who holds that belief, our chances of passing aren't good no matter how many spins we can pull out of."

Mandy Lou put down her soup spoon. "But we can ask for a second check test, if we fail the first. My instructor said so. Surely that improves our odds of success."

"Maybe," Nila replied. "But do you really think that

67

the second check pilot will go against the first's decision? Ann had a second test. She claimed that it was little more than a formality."

"Was Ann a good pilot?" I asked.

"She had been an instructor at an airfield in California," Barbara replied. "In fact, I think that she had been giving lessons for almost three years. She couldn't have held that position that long if she wasn't good."

All of us nodded in agreement.

Mandy Lou picked up her spoon again. "Who was her check pilot?"

"Lieutenant Calley," Nila replied, off-handedly. She began to butter a piece of bread then turned to me. "Aren't you the next person to be tested?"

I nodded.

"Do you know who your check pilot will be?" she asked.

I nodded again and swallowed hard before replying, "Lieutenant Calley."

There were murmurs of sympathy all around the table. I didn't know if that meant that my friends felt sorry for me or if they thought that I was about to fail. I do know that I had completely lost my appetite.

Nila began to give her impressions of Sweetwater to change the subject, and although I tried to participate, I just couldn't concentrate on anything that was being said. I would have to quiz Nila later about Ann's ride to try to figure out what went wrong. I had survived Oleander Court, several ground school classes, and an engine fire. Lieutenant Calley might be determined to fail me. I, however, was just as determined to pass.

Chapter 10

On Friday morning, March 19, the day of my PT test, it was all I could do to concentrate on my assignment in communications class. I kept thinking about what lay ahead of me in the afternoon, mentally running through the checklists to make sure that I at least had that part down pat. I repeatedly checked my watch, amazed that time could move so slowly.

When we broke for lunch, I drank some tea and passed up all food. Not only did I want to be in the best shape for stalls and spins, I was too nervous to eat.

At long last, 1:00 P.M. arrived, and I reported to the ready room as scheduled. I slipped on my parachute and ran through all of the items on each checklist one last time.

Tall, tanned, and fit, Lieutenant Calley strutted into the room 15 minutes late. He picked up a clipboard, nodded in my direction, and without a word headed toward the plane. I followed him out the door.

I did everything that I could to get complete control of myself as I marched toward the Stearman, including patting my locket with Mother's picture and good luck charm. Walking helped relieve some tension and repeating my roommates' good wishes helped a little more. Barbara had insisted that I toss a coin into a shallow wishing well near the mess hall on our way to breakfast this morning. If my wish comes true and I pass my test, my friends will toss me into the well this afternoon, where I am supposed to retrieve my money. If I fail, I will be packing my suitcase within an hour.

I checked my plane carefully as Calley towered over me. I knew that I could pass this part of the test if I concentrated on what I was doing. It was the next part that worried me, because so much depended upon the check pilot's ideal. How long should it take to pull out of a spin or to level the plane's wings? The answers, I was sure, varied from pilot to pilot, and since I was only the second to be tested by Calley, I hadn't the slightest idea of what his expectations might be.

When Lieutenant Calley finally took his place in the cockpit, he gave me my orders. I was to climb to 6,000 feet and fly the traditional pattern once; stall and recover; return to 6,000 feet and do a left-hand spin; go to 7,000 feet and do a right-hand spin; return to the pattern, which I was to do twice; and land. That was a lot to remember in the best of times, and this wasn't one of them. Nila had warned me that part of Ann's problem had been that she couldn't remember all of Calley's directions and that he had refused to repeat them. To solve this problem, I had fastened a notepad to my right thigh after I had entered the cockpit. When Calley had rattled off the directions, I had written them down.

At first, everything went well. After receiving permission to take off, I climbed to 6,000 feet, flew the pattern without any difficulty, stalled, then recovered nicely. Even the left-hand spin went better than I could have hoped.

But just as I was about to relax a little, I felt the stick move. Calley, using his controls, pulled it all the way back and when he hit the rudder, the plane went into another left-hand spin, sharper than anything I would have tried. I was thrown hard against the side of the Stearman, and the blow momentarily stunned me.

"That wasn't part of the test, and you know it!" I shouted into the headset when I regained my senses. "This is my plane! Take your hands off the controls and keep them off!"

Without a word, Calley released the stick. I then stopped the spin and leveled the Stearman, checking my progress by looking over my shoulder to do so. When I thought that I had everything under control, I got back into the pattern. As soon as I reached the spot where the surprise spin had taken place, I checked my notes and completed the test exactly as I had been instructed to do, ending with the best landing that I had ever made.

As I climbed out of the plane and joined Calley on the ground, it was all I could do to even look at him. He made a few marks on a form on his clipboard then glanced in my direction. I tried to read his expression, but I found it impossible to do so. I thought that I saw a flicker of a smile when he spotted my notes, which were still firmly attached to my leg, but that may have been a mistake. He just as easily could have been trying to suppress a sneer.

It wasn't my place to say anything, so I remained silent. Besides, I was afraid of what I might say once I got started. If he said that I had failed, I was sure that I could not hold back a real outburst of my so-called unladylike temper. I had done a fine job and I knew it. I wanted my reward.

"I believe that you have one more task to complete before advancing to the BTs," he said matter-of-factly. "You need to complete a solo flight at night."

"I can't make my solo flight until I pass this check flight. I don't know that I did." Say it, I said to myself. *The least you can do after pulling your despicable stunt is to actually say that I passed, not just hint at it.*

Lieutenant Calley shrugged his shoulders. "You passed."

I smiled slightly, turned, and walked toward the ready room the way I thought a queen might walk. I kept this up until I saw my roommates and Mr. Jacob waiting for me. I then dropped my royal gait and ran to them. "I passed!" I shouted as loudly as I could. "I passed!"

Amid cheers and offers of congratulations, I heard someone cry, "Into the well with her!" We fell in line, with Mr. Jacob bringing up the rear. When we reached our destination, the rest of my classmates, some with cameras in hand, were waiting for me. I'm not sure who threw me in. It doesn't matter. I just know that it was the most wonderful dunking ever. When I found what I thought was my quarter, I held it high in the air, then offered it to Nila, who had helped me so much and would be the next to take a PT test. "From the bottom of my heart," I said, "I wish you the same success."

Nila smiled and took the coin.

Then we fell in line once more and marched to our barracks. I was the first in my class to pass the PT test, living proof that it could be done. Both smiles and renewed hope were visible on every face.

I decided to take my night solo flight the following evening. With a thermos of hot chocolate and a sandwich to sustain me during the flight, I cleared my plans with Mr. Jacob. I was to fly to Midland, Texas, radio the tower to prove that I had made my destination, circle the airport, then return to Avenger. In all, my flight would be about 250 miles round-trip, or approximately three hours long.

Because I had to prove that I could take off, navigate, and land at night, I had to wait at least an hour after the sun set before I could leave Avenger. While I waited for permission to leave, I checked and rechecked every part of the plane. When my number finally came up, I taxied down the runway and headed west.

The flight was beautiful. Lights in small towns and ranch houses glowed below and stars twinkled above. The moon cast shadows on the ground, including a semblance of my PT, and turned my plane's wings into a soft, shimmering shade of silver. Although the air was perfectly still, I could have sworn that I heard music in the distance.

In little over an hour, I saw Midland almost as clearly as I had on previous trips in daylight. The town was surrounded by oil wells, and owners routinely burned off the gas 24 hours a day. From the air, the city looked like a giant birthday cake outlined with huge candles.

After radioing the tower, I headed east. I mentally checked off the names of towns along the way, using them as a trail that would lead to Avenger. When I was certain that my airfield was next, I circled it to get my bearings, then requested permission to land. During the day, I could see the ground clearly, making it possible for me to estimate when I was about to touch the runway, the most difficult part of landing. But at night this is not an easy thing to do, since the runway is lit only with flares. So as I dropped in altitude, I concentrated hard on trying to feel what Mr. Jacob called a cushion of air, an invisible pillow beneath the plane when the aircraft is just above the ground. Meanwhile I kept checking the horizon, which is not an especially easy thing to do in the dark either. When I finally felt the cushion—and it took longer than I thought it would—I set the craft down, brought it to a complete stop, and climbed out of the cockpit.

After securing my plane, I patted one of its wings with great affection. We were parting, the PT and I. As soon as I had filled out the required forms, my primary training would be finished, and I would be embarking on a whole new set of challenges. Whether I was up to them remained to be seen.

Chapter 11

On the morning of March 22, my group began instrument training—something that I had looked forward to for some time—in ground school class. I didn't mind navigating by identifying landforms once I had managed to memorize key sites, but the challenge of finding an exact spot with just the help of a few dials and flying the plane entirely by instrument fascinated me.

Mr. Wright, a navigation expert, took us to the Link trainer room, which had several varieties of flight simulators. Each one was about the size of a small cockpit. Some were open on one side; others were boxes that completely enclosed the student. All had a panel of instruments and a headset.

"Your instructor," Mr. Wright began, pointing to desks that had microphones on them, "will sit outside the trainer and give you orders. He will create a hypothetical situation. You'll react to it using the controls in your trainer, leveling the plane, for example, without the help of the horizon.

He walked over to one of the trainers and took down one of many wreaths that were hanging all around the room. Each wreath, the kind that people hang on their front doors when someone in the family has died, was a circle of black leaves, probably made from silk. The circle was topped with a big black bow with long streamers. He held it high in the air so all could see. "Each one of these," he said, "represents a Link trainer 'crash.' I'm hopeful that the wreaths will impress upon you the fact that it's easy to make mistakes. Here, in our make-believe world, you'll be able to just walk away. Failures in the real world will most likely be deadly.

"Before you can take your check test, you must convince your instructor and me that you have mastered the skills needed to fly under the hood. On test day," he walked over to a desk and picked up a huge piece of black cloth, "a cover will be put over your head and instruments. Your check pilot will get the plane airborne, then turn the controls over to you. You'll fly to a specific site, which will be announced in the air, and return to Avenger without looking at the sky, the horizon, or even a single landmark. If, when you are told that you can remove your cover, Avenger airfield lies directly below, you have passed your test. If you are above anything else, you have failed."

We spent the entire morning trying to get the hang of

instrument flying. When we complained that this was going to be difficult, we were told that the worst was yet to come. After our Link training we would be taught how to "fly the beam," which involved using the Morse Code to navigate, an even greater challenge.

That afternoon, I met Miss Bellows, who was to be my BT instructor. She was about 40 years old, short, and very slender. She wore her long salt-and-pepper hair in a bun, and she dressed from head to toe in denim. She sported red cowboy boots, and numerous silver rings and bracelets that glistened in the sunlight as we walked from the ready room to the plane. She was the only female flight instructor at Avenger, and all business.

"Are you familiar with the BT-13?" she asked.

"No. I've never flown one," I replied.

"It handles very differently than a Stearman," she warned me. "But the checklist is basically the same. That's where we'll start today."

I nodded.

She went through the procedure, reminding me, as Mr. Jacob had, that failure to perform the tests would be enough to send me home. As we went through the list, I studied the plane. It was approximately 30 feet long. I guessed that the wingspan was about 40 feet, which made it a bit larger than the Stearman. It was a sleek-looking aircraft, and I knew that it could reach speeds of up to 180 miles per hour with its 450 horsepower engine. I also knew that the advanced classes were not fond of the craft. They thought that it was a difficult plane to fly; it literally shook in the air if pushed too hard. In fact, they called it the Vibrator, or worse yet, Bucket of Bolts. The BT had a greenhouse-type canopy, which was a mixed blessing. An enclosed cockpit was more comfortable, especially at high altitudes, but it limited visibility.

After receiving permission to take off, we climbed to 7,000 feet. Miss Bellows flew a now very familiar pattern. She took the plane up to stall it, and shortly after she put it into a right-hand spin. When the plane began to turn, it shook so much I thought that parts of it would fly off. It responded more slowly than a Stearman did when she pulled it out of the spin, and it took her a long time to level the plane. This aircraft had more size and speed, but it did not handle as well as my PT. In short, it would be hard work to fly it.

"Did you notice the difference, Elizabeth, between this plane and your Stearman? How it reacts in a stall and spin?"

"Yes."

"If you become a ferry pilot," she said, "you will probably fly more BT-13s or the newer version, the BT-15, than any other plane. For some reason, BTs have been requested by all army air force bases that have pilot training, and there are a lot of them."

I wasn't especially pleased to hear that.

"Tomorrow I want you to repeat what I did today. Now concentrate on my landing. The BT's speed is nearly double that of the PT's, so you must make some adjustments. I'll describe each step. Tomorrow you can impress me with how quickly you learn."

I listened carefully. Like Mr. Jacob, Miss Bellows was a good teacher, and by the time we touched down, I was certain that with her help I could master the Bucket of Bolts.

My lesson had taken a little longer than usual, so I was one of the last women to enter the mess hall that evening. The room, often full of laughter and conversation, was strangely quiet, and tense students with grim faces surrounded the tables. Few women were actually eating; most were simply picking at their food. As I went through the line, I tried to figure out what was wrong.

I took my usual spot across from Mandy Lou. "Why is everyone so quiet?"

"You haven't heard?"

I shook my head. "I just finished my lesson."

Mandy Lou took a deep breath. "Cornelia Fort died in an airplane crash yesterday."

"Who?"

"Cornelia Fort, a ferrying pilot in Nancy Love's program."

When I still didn't respond, Nila, who was seated to my right, plunged in. "Fort was the first pilot Love recruited when she set up her program. Cornelia had been a flight instructor in Hawaii when the war began, and she had actually witnessed Japan's surprise attack on Pearl Harbor—from the air. Fort had thousands of hours of flight time, and she was probably one of the best, if not *the* best, pilots that Love had."

"How did she die?" I asked.

"According to rumors," Nila replied, "Fort was flying in formation with six ferrying pilots, all men. They were delivering BTs to an army air force base in Dallas. One of the pilots pulled out of the formation too quickly, and in the process, he hit one of Fort's wings. The blow forced her plane into a deadly spin, and she couldn't regain control."

Heartsick, for even those of us who didn't know Cornelia felt as if we had lost a sister, most of us left the mess hall early, leaving behind large portions of our evening meal. As Nila and I walked back to our barracks, I wondered aloud if Love's program and ours were in jeopardy, now that a fatality had occurred.

"Much depends," Nila replied, "upon exactly what happened. I'm sure there will be an investigation. If Cornelia was at fault, and I doubt that she was from what we have heard so far, the naysayers just might get their way. After telling us that what they're doing is for our own good, they'll close down both ferrying programs and send us home."

We stopped at the wishing well, each of us fishing coins from our pockets, tossing the quarters and dimes into the water one at a time. "If this had happened at the very beginning of the ferrying program," Nila continued, "I'm certain that our training would have been canceled. Many Americans become upset at the very idea of women supporting a war effort, let alone dying while doing so. Now, in part because our losses have been so high on the battlefield, the public realizes that we're in a very bloody conflict that will require great sacrifice, even the lives of some women, if we are to win."

She pulled a few more coins from her pocket, again tossing them into the pool, one after another. "Another thing that makes it different now than when the program began is the fact that many women are at risk besides us. Female nurses are tending wounded soldiers near combat lines, and women journalists are following our troops as they march toward the enemy. Some women have even joined auxiliaries of the armed services." She paused and turned to face me. "My sister is a Wac. Did you know that?"

I shook my head.

"She wants to go overseas, and I hope . . . anyway, what makes Fort's death and the others that will follow a little easier to accept is the knowledge that all of us—nurses, correspondents, Wacs, and pilots—volunteered for our duties. We chose to put our lives at risk, unlike thousands of young men who were not given a choice."

We stood at the well for several minutes before resuming our march in silence. The day had been especially long and trying.

Chapter 12

All of us were very cautious for at least two weeks following Cornelia's death. We checked and double-checked everything, paid careful attention to our instructors' directions, and pretended that tragedy could not strike twice.

During that time, my lessons in the BT-13 progressed as well as could be expected, although, to be honest, my attention was on the AT-Texan, the next trainer. The advanced students were so in love with this plane that their instructors had to practically drag them out of the aircraft at the end of their flying sessions. According to these women, the AT was a fast beauty—it could fly more than 200 miles per hour!—and it responded quickly to any movement at the control panel. I couldn't wait to fly it, but in order to do so, I had to master the Vibrator. So I tried hard to concentrate on the task at hand and get it over with as soon as possible.

Link training also progressed well. I actually liked it and, unlike my first ground school classes, I looked forward to going to school now. In fact, if I hadn't wanted to fly so badly, I would have seriously considered becoming a Link instructor, for which there was a great demand.

Although I was having success in the trainer, Mandy Lou was having a lot of trouble. She ended up in one of the trainers that is completely enclosed. I knew that she was afraid of the dark. I also knew that her instructor sensed her fear. But instead of helping her overcome it, he pushed onward, mumbling something about "If you *really* want to graduate . . ."

Now that I was experiencing progress in the air and on land, I had a little more time to write home. But try as I might, I couldn't send enough letters to keep Jimmy happy.

April 6, 1943

Dear Liz,

At last, a letter from you. Thanks!

Everything is fine here.

My all-school skit was a great success. Mr. Blanchard, the ninth-grade English teacher, liked it and my performance so much that he asked me to think about trying out for the Thespians' next play, which will be given in our auditorium in July. I don't know what play they're going to do or what my part will be. I don't really care. The important thing is that my acting career has begun!

Uncle Wilbert stopped by last week. He had heard about Cornelia Fort's crash, and he was wondering if you had come to your senses and were headed home. I told him that I didn't think that you were quite ready for charm school yet. I said that you were having too much fun. Then I showed him one of the pictures that you had sent—the one in which you are coming out of the wishing well and your hair and clothes are a mess.

Oh, how I wish you could have been here to see his reaction! He actually groaned. Then he said, and I'm quoting from my journal, "That *can't* be my niece. My niece is a Sterling, and Sterlings don't do things like that."

I held the picture closer to his face and said, "But it is your niece, sir. Don't you recognize her eyes and her smile? Well, her wet hair covers up her eyes, but certainly you recognize her smile."

Our sophisticated uncle said, of all possibly clever things, "Ugh!" Then he got panicky. "You haven't shown that to anyone else, have you?"

I told him that Father had taken all of your pictures to work and had shown them to everyone who came in. Then Wilbert groaned again. It was just wonderful!

Anyway, now I really want to know what you're doing. The bigger the challenge, the more I'll like it. I want to do an encore for Wilbert the next time he comes. So write as soon as possible and tell me everything!

Love from all,
Jim

P.S. Father is so proud of you and, believe me, Mother would have been too.

Chapter 13

In mid-April the first class of ferrying pilots, 22 in all, was ready to receive its wings. The rest of us, which included the class immediately in front of us and the two classes behind us, were expected to march in formation for review before the graduation for General Arnold, the commander of the entire army air force, and Jackie Cochran herself.

Because we still didn't have uniforms, we decided to march in our ground school clothes. To make our simple outfits more impressive, we purchased khaki hats, the kind soldiers wear with their dress clothes. The hats were not my favorite style. They reminded me of upside-down canoes, and they were hard to keep in place without the help of half a dozen bobby pins. Still, when I looked at my classmates, I had to admit that the caps really did add a little polish.

The ceremony that evening was patriotic and very emotional. Major Hogan gave a rousing introduction about women risking their lives to help win the war. General Arnold followed him with a summary of where the war effort stood—our soldiers had taken an important pass in Libya only days before—then went on to express our all-out determination to win. After that, we rose, faced the flag, and recited the Pledge of Allegiance. This was followed by the singing of "God Bless America," a song that always brings tears to my eyes.

When we were seated, we turned our attention to the graduates. Everyone in the room was well aware of what they had accomplished and the history that they had made. Several shed tears of joy when they received their certificates and silver wings from General Arnold. While I watched the proud graduates march across the stage before us, I dreamed of the not-too-distant day when I would be standing on stage with Arnold and Cochran, shaking their hands and awaiting my orders.

The following day, ground school classes went well enough, but we had a disaster in the afternoon. When I returned to my room after a late flight lesson, I found my classmates waiting for me. Barbara, who was sitting on the edge of her bed, was the center of attention. She was pale, disheveled, bruised, and for the first time that I could recall, crying. Two women from the room next to us sat beside her, trying to comfort her.

I immediately went to Barbara and knelt before her. "Barbara! What happened? Are you all right?"

She just shook her head, trying hard to get her emotions under control.

When it was clear that she couldn't answer, I rose and looked around the room. "What's going on?"

Nila spoke up. "Barbara lost control of her plane while she was trying to do a spin. She had to parachute to safety."

"What?" I looked back at Barbara. "Is this true?"

Barbara nodded. "But . . . but that's not all," she said, dabbing at her eyes with wads of tissues.

"What do you mean, that's not all?"

"My . . . my plane had been tampered with. After I had been picked up and . . . and . . told to return to my barracks, I found Nila." She paused, wiping away more tears. "We went back to look at the plane. My rudder cables had been cut."

Old fears quickly grabbed hold of me, and I felt dizzy and sick to my stomach. Hoping that there had been some kind of mistake, I questioned Barbara. "Are you absolutely sure about the cables?"

"Yes, oh, yes," Barbara said softly. "Someone tried to kill me." Then she started to cry again.

"But that just can't be," I argued, trying hard to make the problem just disappear.

"Barbara's right, Liz", Nila said matter-of-factly. "One cable was so badly damaged in the crash that we couldn't tell one way or another, but the other cable was definitely cut half way through. The break was smooth for part of the way, then really ragged. I think that it snapped when she hit the rudder to make the plane go into a spin."

It had been more than a month since we had had any

trouble, and I had assumed that whoever was behind the incidents had quit. "Why would this person—this monster—do this now?" I wondered aloud.

"We've been talking about that," Mandy Lou replied. "We think that the vandal set out to destroy the ferrying program from the very beginning. There were some strange incidents even before we arrived in Houston, but some of the first planes were in such poor shape that no one was certain if they had been tampered with or had fallen apart on their own. Then Nila had trouble and you had a fire. I think that the vandal assumed that we would become so frightened after those incidents that we would quit. But we didn't. He couldn't arrange more so-called accidents after that because we were watching our planes more closely, and someone might have spotted him tampering with the trainers. So he had to wait awhile, until our guard was down." She looked at Barbara. "Did you check your plane carefully?"

Barbara looked at the floor. "After we left Houston, I thought that the danger was behind us. I looked, but not very carefully."

Mandy Lou sighed. "I haven't been especially vigilant either." She paused, as if gathering her thoughts. "Maybe he believed that it was safe enough to vandalize another plane after all this time, or maybe graduation last night upset him and drove him back into action again. Who knows?"

"But who would do such a thing?" I asked, mentally running through a list of names of those who worked on the base and had been with us in Houston.

"It could be anyone who has access to the planes," Nila replied, "a mechanic who thinks that women shouldn't fly, a groundskeeper who's a Nazi sympathizer, a spy, or even a professional saboteur. 'He' could even be more than one person."

Anger flashed in Nila's eyes. "Unfortunately my suspicions were correct," she said, "and my solution was wrong. We certainly can't rely on checking our planes to keep us safe anymore. On the other hand, if we report the incidents, the army will stop our training while investigators try to get to the bottom of this frightening mess. That could take months, and there is no guarantee that the army will catch the vandal—or vandals. In the meantime, they get what they want: the program will come to a halt, even if it is only for a short while."

"Also," said Mandy Lou, "if we report this and word about this crash gets into the papers—and it will—many of us will be withdrawn from the program. When my mother hears about engine fires and severed cables, she'll faint. As soon as she comes to, my parents will come to Sweetwater to get me. I'll bet that I won't be the only one whose parents will end a ferrying career real fast. For every girl who leaves, the monsters behind all of this can claim a victory."

"But we have to report the tampering," Barbara said. "I could have been killed today. We've had at least three incidents now, and fortunately, they were all near misses. These vandals show no sign of stopping, and the next incident could be deadly." She looked around the room.

"Any of you could be next. And," looking at Nila, then me, "just because you've already been through one accident doesn't mean that you couldn't have another. I don't want to die, and I don't want any of you to die either."

I was well aware that anyone could be a victim, even an instructor, since we didn't have assigned planes. Instead, we took the first trainer available, whatever the mechanics thought was ready to fly. "I'm not ready to report this, yet," I said. "I'd rather try to find some way to keep the vandals away from our planes."

"How are we going to do that?" Mandy Lou asked. "How can we even figure out who we're supposed to frighten? If we talk to everyone we might suspect, and insult a lot of people in the process, someone will tell Major Hogan about what's going on. The result will be an investigation. If we check our planes any more than we do now to let the culprits know that we are looking for trouble, our instructors will become suspicious, and that will also result in an investigation. But reporting the incident and checking our planes are the only things that I can think of doing, and neither is a good solution. This is so frustrating!"

"If only there was some way that we could keep an eye on the planes," Barbara said. "But the mechanics do most of the work at night, when we're sleeping. Besides, even if we could go without sleep, we can't be wandering around the hangars at all hours without arousing suspicion."

"Maybe we could hire someone," Mandy Lou

suggested. "I could get money from Daddy without having to give too many explanations. What do private investigators cost? Does anyone know?"

"A private investigator at Avenger might scare off the vandals," Nila said. "But how would we get an investigator onto the base without alerting Hogan to the problem? I'm afraid that's out too."

"There has to be a way," Barbara said. "There just has to be. Nineteen of us should be able to come up with something."

"I think there is a way," I said, running an idea through my head. "What if we have an investigation of a totally different kind . . . one that's not aimed at finding the vandals . . . but might eventually do so anyway?"

"I think that you have to explain that," Mandy Lou said.

"My father is a newspaper editor. He has lots of friends and relatives in the business, including a cousin on a Dallas paper, a Mr. Byrd, if I remember right. What if Father asks his cousin to do a favor, an exclusive, in-depth article about the ferrying program? Father could tell him about our concerns, and I'm certain that they would remain a secret. A reporter who says that he wants to do a positive article about us could easily persuade Major Hogan to let him come onto the base and ask lots of questions. The journalist could be here at unexpected times, conducting interviews and taking pictures every time he turns around. The reporter would get a good story—after all, the ferrying program is interesting— and we might get peace of mind. *If* the reporter finds out who is responsible for the sabotage, the newspaper gets a *really* good story, and we haven't put our program at risk because the danger would then be behind us."

Mandy Lou studied me for a moment. "Are you sure that your father would let you stay if you told him about everything that has happened? Mine certainly wouldn't. And would your father keep the vandalism a secret?"

"Father lets me make my own decisions," I replied. "He would not make me leave the program, nor would he betray us by reporting anything that I said in confidence."

"Liz's idea could work," Nila said. "A reporter's presence just might scare off the vandals. Whether he can figure out who's behind the tampering remains to be seen. By going this route, though, we may give up any chance of catching the culprits."

There was a murmur of voices now as the women discussed the plan among themselves. After more than an hour of debate, they agreed to bring in a journalist.

I then headed to the nearest phone to call Father.

When I returned, I talked to Barbara. I was afraid that she might be thinking about quitting, and I didn't want whoever had tampered with her plane to have any success. At the same time, I understood Barbara's feelings. To help her deal with her fear, I suggested that she ask for a few days off. I hoped that this would be enough time for Barbara to once again become the confident, cheerful person we had come to know and love. I also fervently hoped that by having two or three days of incident-free flying, we could convince Barbara that the danger was behind us. If, on the other hand, we had accidents of any kind, I knew that Barbara—and probably a few more— would quit. Our reporter couldn't get here soon enough.

Chapter 14

"You can come out from under the hood now, Elizabeth," said Lieutenant Hughes, my check pilot. "Look at the ground below and see if you recognize anything."

I hoped that what I saw wasn't a surprise. I had spent the last two hours in the air flying a BT-13 to Ft. Worth and back to Avenger entirely by instrument. If I wasn't above my favorite airfield, I would just die. When my eyes finally adjusted to the sunlight and I looked below and realized that I was right where I wanted to be, I was so happy I actually let out a loud "Whoopee!"

"Congratulations!" Lieutenant Hughes shouted. "Circle once or twice if you want, then land."

As soon as I had secured the aircraft, I headed straight for Miss Bellows' office to make plans for my cross-country flight. This would be my last BT test, and I was eager to get it behind me so that I could *finally* fly an advanced trainer.

"Your destination," Miss Bellows said, "is Blythe, California, which is just inside the state's eastern border." She picked up a map, spread it out on her desk, then traced my route. "The Sweetwater-Blythe round trip is nine hundred miles. You'll have to fly over the Continental Divide and the Sacramento Mountains, the highest of which is over twelve thousand feet. This will involve a lot of climbing, and the danger of stalling is very real. Also, instead of passing over cities with clearly marked water towers, you'll cross vast deserts that have few easily identifiable landmarks to help you find your way. In addition, this is a long flight—almost five hours in the air to reach Blythe—with no breaks." She looked at me. "It's a hard test, Elizabeth, so plot your course carefully."

Two of my classmates who had failed their BT cross-country test had warned me about this trip. One of the students had lost her way, and when her fuel supply ran low as she crisscrossed the landscape looking for clues to her location, she was forced to land—in Mexico. Another student couldn't find Blythe. She also committed the unpardonable sin in the ferrying program of turning back rather than landing as soon as possible and then requesting help. Not only are we forbidden to turn back—and potentially get even more lost than we already are—we are not allowed, once we make an emergency landing, to take off again. Usually a plane suffers some damage during such a landing, particularly if it took place on a rough site, and the aircraft needs repair work as well as an experienced pilot to get it back into the air.

"Flying long distances is very stressful," Miss Bellows added, "so when you reach Blythe, land. Make arrangements to spend the night on the base and return the following morning."

On April 30, I reported to the ready room for my last-minute instructions. After reviewing my map one last time and examining my plane—very thoroughly!—I took off.

I had little cause for concern until I neared Midland. In the distance, I noticed a long line of clouds, which meant that I was approaching a front. The weather forecast had not included a storm warning. However, I was well aware that forecasters weren't always right, especially in the spring when storms sometimes seemed to pop up out of nowhere. I thought that I might be able to fly over the clouds, so I continued westward. But the closer I got to the front, the more the clouds appeared to rise ever higher in the sky, churning as they did so. When I looked at the ground, I saw trees bending low in the wind and dust swirling across the landscape.

Even so, I was determined to go on. Shortly before I reached the edge of the cloud cover, I started to climb. The air was surprisingly turbulent, rocking my plane from side to side, making my stomach queasy and me very nervous. I tried breathing deeply to relieve my tension. It didn't work. Then I hit an air pocket, and my plane dropped several hundred feet. Suddenly I was six inches above my seat and my safety belt was straining to hold me down as my BT dropped faster than I did. I didn't breathe until I hit the bottom of the pocket. I needed time to calm down and re-evaluate the situation, so I turned my plane around and flew away from the storm.

After a lengthy debate with myself, I decided to try to climb over the clouds once more. But the air was so choppy now that I could barely keep the BT level, and at times I felt as if I was in a small boat in a big storm as I was tossed to and fro. When I climbed higher to get out of the turbulence, my plane began to shake and then it stalled. I recovered as quickly as I could, and turned back once more.

Refusing to give up, I steeled myself for one more attempt, this time under the clouds. As I slid beneath their flat bottoms, they began to release their moisture. Sprinkles were followed by rain drops that were followed by sheets of water. The downpour was so heavy at times that I could barely see where I was going. Bolts of lightning appeared in front and behind me, and the air was so charged with electricity that the hair on my neck and arms actually stood up. I knew now that I was in great danger. I also knew that I was in a lot of trouble for trying to fly through a storm.

After radioing the Midland tower to report my location, I began to drop as quickly as I could to make an emergency landing. As the winds buffeted my BT and torrents of rain washed over me, I fully understood why experienced pilots *never* tried to outmaneuver a storm. "Only an arrogant fool," I muttered, "would try."

Knowing that I had several things in my favor, I calmed down a bit. First, I had my plane under control.

Second, I knew that open fields lay below, that is, if I remembered the landscape correctly. In addition, I had been drilled on every kind of landing by Joe and my instructors. So I circled and circled, waiting to feel a cushion of air as I neared the earth, trying to remember everything that I had been taught about landing on a short runway in crosswinds and keeping my plane level. When I finally touched the ground, I bounced quite a bit, then came to a halt in what I thought was an old hayfield.

Reaching safety did not solve all of my problems, though. Believing that I would be sent packing for trying to fly through the squall, I was very angry—at myself. "Elizabeth Margaret Erickson," I shouted, "you've ruined everything—everything! Months of planning and hard work, and you just threw it all away." A bolt of lightning flashed in the sky, as if emphasizing my point. "What will you say when they ask why you did this? What *can* you say?"

I ranted until my anger was spent then tried to settle back into the cockpit for what I knew would be a long wait. Although I tried to think of something other than my current predicament, the events of the last hour kept creeping back into my thoughts, mixed, strangely enough, with bits and pieces of Wilbert's story about Mother's last flight. I couldn't help comparing the two situations, and now that I had been through such an ordeal, I was more confused than ever as to why my mother, an experienced and cautious pilot, would have deliberately flown into a storm. Yet apparently she had. "Why?" I asked. "Why? Why? Why?"

About half an hour had passed when some of the bits and pieces fell into place, and I finally realized that I had been lied to—by an arrogant fool. Now I was awash in mixed emotions: rage and relief. I was overwhelmed with questions. The downpour had ended, so I climbed out of the cockpit and onto the sod so that I might walk off some of my pent-up energy. I paced back and forth, splashed through mud puddles, and spent the next three hours trying to figure out what I was going to do.

I still hadn't reached any conclusions when my rescuers arrived, racing across the field toward me in an army jeep. The first man to get out was the mechanic. He carried a large tool box, and he would examine the plane and determine if and when it could be flown. The other man, whose face I couldn't see at first, would fly the BT and me back to Avenger when it was possible to do so. As he got out of the jeep, I groaned. It was none other than Lieutenant Calley.

Because the sod had acted as a cushion for my landing and had also prevented me from becoming muddied in, my plane was in remarkably good condition. Also, unlike emergency landings forced by mechanical failure, which required lots of repairs, there had been nothing wrong with the plane before I landed. So after only a few tests and minor adjustments to the BT's landing gear, the craft was ready to fly again.

Calley piloted the BT for the entire flight, during which neither of us said a word. When we finally landed at Avenger, I climbed out of the cockpit and began to walk toward my barracks. "Not so fast, Elizabeth," Calley shouted. "I want to talk to you!"

When we were seated in the ready room, he looked me in the eye, then spoke very softly, which to be honest, surprised me. "Why did you try to fly through the storm?"

"I know that I should have landed right away. I made a serious error in judgment. I'll leave the program, if that's what you want."

"You didn't answer my question, Elizabeth. I want to know why you tried to do the nearly impossible."

I shrugged my shoulders.

Calley waited and waited for a reply. When none came, he tried a different approach. "What do you have on the chain around your neck?"

His question startled me. "A good luck charm," I replied, "and a locket."

"Whose picture is in the locket?"

"Isn't that rather personal? What does that have to do with the program?"

"I think that it has a lot to do with the program. I think that the locket has a picture of your mother in it."

"How . . . ?"

"I've done a lot of checking on you. From the beginning, you've wanted to succeed more than any of the other students, always trying to do things just a bit better than anyone else. I wanted to know why for reasons I'll explain in a minute. During my investigation, I learned that your mother was piloting a plane when it crashed and she was killed. She was your first instructor, and I think that you're trying to help her reputation by proving how well you, her student, can do."

I didn't want to discuss this, especially not now. Calley, however, wasn't about to stop talking. He leaned forward to emphasize his next point. "That's a heavy burden, Elizabeth, and I think that it's time for you to put it down. I'm reasonably certain that your mother would want you to live your own life, not try to redeem hers."

I was afraid that if I started to talk, I might say too much, so I refused to comment on Calley's observations. Besides, I just wanted to end this conversation and be alone for a while. But Calley still wasn't about to let me go. "You're one of the best pilots in the program," he said. "John Jacob brought you to my attention after he had given you two lessons, and I've been watching you ever since. I was near the runway when your plane caught fire. I was so impressed with how you handled yourself that day that I asked to be your check pilot."

"*Why* would you do that?"

"I wanted to see how much spunk you had." He smiled. "I soon learned. Part of my job is to pick out a few pilots for a special program. Some of the planes that will be ferried will be experimental planes, containing the latest and best equipment. Our enemies would like to know what that equipment is like, and spies can provide the answers. A few women will be trained to fly these planes. These pilots must also be prepared to guard the aircraft if need be. You might be a good addition to the chosen few if you'd stop taking chances to try to improve your mother's reputation."

I looked up at him in surprise. "Then I'm not out of the program?"

"No, at least not yet. Actually, what you did today makes you a stronger candidate than ever in the sense that you proved that you are not easily frightened nor do you give up without a fight. But I want you to think about what I've said. You have to know when to take chances and when not to. The decisions should have nothing to do with your mother."

He looked at me again, and this time I thought I noted a little sympathy in his expression. "I know that you need rest," he said, "so before you go I should warn you that a reporter from Dallas is here to do a story about the ferrying program. He especially wants to talk to you because you're the youngest student. I think he's in the hangar area. If you want to avoid him, I'd suggest taking a roundabout route to your room."

I was tired all right, but the thought that Father's cousin was already on base was a great relief. I had no intention of avoiding him. Actually, I was eager to meet him. Maybe, just maybe, everything was going to be all right.

Chapter 15

When I found Mr. Byrd, he was interviewing Barbara. I stood in the shadows and studied him for a moment. He was of medium height and build. His dark hair was combed straight back, and his navy suit had nary a wrinkle. Several notepads, a pile of pens, and a large camera lay on the table before him. As he talked to Barbara, he studied her very carefully, as if weighing every word she said.

I already knew a little about Mr. Byrd, since Father had told me about his Texas relatives when I asked him to find a reporter for us. He said that the Byrds traced their ancestry all the way back to Jamestown and that the Byrd name is highly regarded in Texas, for some of the first family members to arrive in the area had fought for Texas's independence more than 100 years ago. Father didn't tell me that Mr. Byrd would be especially handsome.

As soon as Barbara left, I walked to the table. "Mr. David Byrd? I'm Elizabeth Erickson."

He rose, turned toward me, and offered his hand. "I'm so pleased to meet you at last. Actually, I'm David Byrd, Jr. My father sends his regrets. He is unable to work on this story now. I was in my father's office when your father called, and I volunteered to do this piece. I'm so glad that I did. This story promises to be wonderful." He pointed to a chair. "Please, take a seat. There is so much I want to ask you."

I did as he asked and filled him in to the best of my knowledge on all that had happened so far.

"Are you aware of any instances of sabotage at the ferrying bases?" he asked.

His question took me aback. "Why, no. I guess I just thought that we were the only ones."

He shook his head. "I have some friends asking questions at the four bases, very quietly, you understand, and they think that sabotage may be a problem elsewhere as well. You do know that Jackie Cochran's plane, the first one that she ferried from Canada to England, had been tampered with."

"No!"

"One of my sources told me that someone broke a window and fiddled with the instruments. I understand that she discovered all of the damage on a routine check before she took off. It wasn't the best way to begin, though, that's for sure."

He looked at a small calendar that lay next to his camera. "I'll be in and out at all hours from now on. That, hopefully, will make your vandals too apprehensive to do much of anything. If you can think of anything else I might do to help, please let me know."

We shook hands once again as I prepared to leave. I knew that Mr. Byrd wasn't a miracle worker, but I believed that because of his presence, we had a better than even chance of stopping our vandals. It wasn't a perfect solution, but it would do for now.

Chapter 16

The month of May was very busy. After passing my second attempt at a cross-country flight to Blythe, I was assigned to the AT program. Everything that the previous classes had told us about the advanced trainers was true. They were a joy to fly; sleek, powerful, and best of all, unlike the BTs, they didn't shake and rattle when pushed a bit. I spent every spare minute possible practicing. I was no longer worried about passing. Flying a pattern or finding my way by instrument or landforms had become routine by now. Also, after all of the frightening and upsetting incidents that I had faced and survived, I felt more confident than ever. I practiced because I just couldn't get enough of flying the AT.

Meanwhile, I also tried to spend as much time as possible with Mr. Byrd. I enjoyed watching him take pictures from many different angles and pop out from behind planes at unexpected times, giving some mechanics a real scare. He also tried to record the faces of everyone who went near a plane. Although we couldn't say for certain that his presence was responsible (our vandals might have gotten transferred or decided to take a break for a while), we didn't have a single accident during the entire month of May, which, needless to say, was a tremendous relief.

My last lessons in navigation were also going well. Besides landforms and instruments, pilots had one more tool to help them find runways. Control towers all over the country sent out two Morse Code signals, dot dash (the letter *A*) and dash dot (the letter *N*) from their airports. The radio signals overlapped above a narrow strip of airspace leading to the runways where they produced a humming noise, which was called "the beam." To find the beam, we zigzagged back and forth in the air until we heard the dots and dashes and then concentrated on finding the hum in between. At first I couldn't hear the unique sound, and I had to learn to listen very carefully to locate the beam. Even so, I enjoyed the challenge. It was a bit like finding a missing piece to a puzzle.

By the end of the month, I had passed my AT check test and cross-country flight. After yet another dunking in the wishing well, I was entitled to wear red socks with my ground school clothes, a not-too-subtle sign of my accomplishments. I still had several classes to pass, but I knew that my goal was in sight. On June 15, I would receive my wings.

From the beginning, Father and Jimmy had been confident that I would become a ferrying pilot, and they had promised to attend my graduation ceremonies even before I had been accepted into the program. Now that my special day was fast approaching, Jimmy was making plans for a celebration in Sweetwater.

May 30, 1943

Dear Liz,

I can't believe that your graduation day is so close! Everything has been arranged on this end. We'll be taking the train to Dallas. Father bought our tickets today. Mr. Byrd has offered to meet us at the station in Dallas and drive us to Sweetwater. He was planning to attend the graduation ceremony anyway. We're going to stay at the Blue Bonnet for three nights, June 14, 15, and 16. We'll arrive about eight o'clock on the fourteenth, so we won't be able to see you until the day you graduate.

I have three surprises for you. One is really great, the other is awful, and I don't know what to call the last one.

First, the good surprise. Father asked Joe if he would like to attend your graduation as our guest, and he said yes! I honestly think that he is at least as excited as I am, and he's told everyone in Chippewa that he's going to see you get your wings.

The bad surprise is that Uncle Wilbert is coming too. He didn't give us a choice. He just said that he's going to join us. I don't understand why he's so interested now. Remember how awful he was when we first talked about you becoming a ferry pilot?

The third surprise is the enclosed letter from the Mayo Clinic. It arrived two weeks ago. The letter was addressed to "The Family of Mrs. Margaret Erickson," so I opened it. After I read the letter I gave it to Father. He has been very different ever since. I can't describe it, really. I asked if I could send the letter to you, and he said that I should. I don't quite know how to say this, but I think that the letter has some great significance and that you'll know what it is.

Sorry to end on such a serious note.

Can't wait to see you!

Love,
Jim

Jimmy was right. After reading the letter, I realized what it meant. I also knew exactly what I would do with the information, and more important, what the information could do for my father, brother, and me. A showdown was in the works.

Chapter 17

Mr. Sterling is in room 226, Miss," the night clerk at the Blue Bonnet Hotel informed me. "Do you want me to ring his room for you?"

"No," I replied. "I want to surprise my uncle." I turned to Barbara, who had driven me to Sweetwater. "I don't know how long this will take."

"Are you sure that you don't want me to come with you, Liz? I know that this is your problem, but I could at least give you moral support, and I promise to keep everything that I hear a secret. Girl Scout's honor," she added as she raised her right hand.

"Thanks," I replied, "but I'd rather do this alone."

I climbed the stairs slowly, organizing my thoughts one last time. When I stood in front of room 226, I paused a moment before knocking loudly. In less than 10 seconds, the door swung open, and there stood Uncle Wilbert, with, to put it mildly, a very surprised look on his face.

"Why . . . why . . . Liz! I didn't expect to see you tonight! Well . . . come in! Come in!" he shouted as he stepped aside, bowed slightly, and made a sweeping gesture with his right arm. And let me congratulate you. You know, I didn't think that you could become a ferry pilot, but you proved me wrong. Imagine that! I'm so proud of you."

Without as much as a smile or a nod, I entered his room.

"Please, Liz, take a seat by the window. Fortunately, I haven't even begun to unpack, so the room is still presentable." As he sat down across from me, he finally noticed my somber mood. "Are you all right, Liz? Should I get you a glass of water or something? You seem so . . . so . . . different, so grown-up somehow."

"This isn't a social call, Uncle Wilbert. You and I have a very serious matter to discuss."

I saw a flicker of apprehension cross his face before he forced a smile. "This isn't the time to talk about a serious matter, whatever that could be. This is the time to talk about accomplishments. So," he said, as he leaned forward in his chair, "let's do something special. Let's go down to the coffee shop and have a treat, a hot-fudge sundae with all the trimmings: whipped cream, chopped nuts, and a cherry on top. You can fill me in on all that's happened."

"Last April," I said, ignoring his invitation, "while flying to California I foolishly tried to get around a thunderstorm. I attempted to go over the storm twice, and when I couldn't keep my plane level, I tried to fly beneath the clouds, an effort that could have resulted in disaster." I looked him straight in the eye now. "I was very lucky. I was able to make an emergency landing without too much difficulty. As soon as I was safe, I raved at myself for taking such a chance. I wouldn't have attempted to beat the storm if I hadn't been trying to prove that I was capable of flying anything anywhere anytime."

I paused for a moment, studying Wilbert's reactions. He was wide-eyed and hanging on every word I uttered. "My experience in that storm," I continued, "convinced me that only a fool would knowingly try to fly in such weather. So it made me wonder why Mother would have tried to do so. She wasn't a fool. She didn't have anything to prove either, nor was there a crisis at home that needed her immediate attention."

I leaned forward to emphasize my next point. "More important, she had every reason to be as careful as possible. For some time, Joe had been talking about taking in a partner again so that he didn't have to work so hard. Mother and I had talked about using the rest of her inheritance money to join the business and eventually become the owners of the airfield. Mother's main concern was how people would react to women running the field and giving lessons. She believed that we would have to prove ourselves at every turn, and that meant *never* taking risks."

"That's why when she crashed," I paused to steady my voice, "I was so devastated. Not only had I lost Mother, whom I dearly loved, I thought that she had betrayed me by taking a foolish chance. By deliberately flying into the storm, she had cast doubt upon her qualifications as a pilot, and indirectly, because she had trained me, my qualifications as well.

"When the ferrying program came along, it was as if I had been given a second chance. I could hardly believe it. I could prove myself in the program, and with the best training in the world behind me, hope to find a job in aviation when the war ended."

Wilbert leaned forward in his chair again. "I'm not sure why you're telling me this, Liz. What does it have to do with me?"

I pulled the letter from the Mayo Clinic from my purse. "Jimmy sent this to me two weeks ago. It seems that the doctor who examined Mother had promised to send a written report to our home. For some reason his report got pushed aside, but when someone at the clinic found it and realized its importance, it was sent to us. It proves that Mother was a diabetic." I handed the letter to Wilbert.

He skimmed it, sighed, then leaned back in his chair. "It's true, Liz. Your mother was diagnosed as a diabetic the day she died. I always wondered if the clinic had sent the doctor's report afterward."

When he saw the look on my face—pure contempt— he began to defend himself. "Look, I was going to tell you, since this puts you and Jimmy at greater risk now, and both of you should be watching for symptoms. But I thought that you had about as much as you could handle when your Mother died, so I decided to wait until I thought that you were better able to deal with more bad news."

I shook my head. "You've had two years to give us that news. I can't recall that you ever even hinted at test results. After all, one of us might have told someone, and the family's secret would have been out. That's not your only lie, though. You said that Mother was flying the Cruiser when it crashed. That's not true. You were the pilot."

Now Wilbert stared at me, barely breathing. Color drained from his face until his skin was as gray as his hair. "Margaret was the pilot," he insisted matter-of-factly.

I shook my head again.

"You just don't want to admit that she was a poor pilot, Liz."

"When I sat in my BT in the field, I *knew* that Mother wouldn't have tried to beat a storm. It wasn't worth the risk. I couldn't prove it then, although I tried hard to find some way. But when I got the letter, I had the evidence I needed to show that Mother wasn't the pilot. I can't tell you how many times Mother had lectured me—for all to hear—about safety and about not flying when I was upset. The news from the doctors that day would have been devastating. She wouldn't have piloted any plane immediately after that even in the best of all weather conditions.

"In fact, I even wondered why she got into the Cruiser if she knew that a storm was coming. The letter answered that question too. The doctor referred to a phone call made by Mother requesting a written report of the lab tests. From the time mentioned in the letter, she must have called from the airfield while you were checking the last-minute weather report. She got into the Cruiser unaware that a storm was on the horizon because you didn't tell her about the danger that lay ahead."

"Liz, be reasonable. Why would I lie about the accident?"

"You lied because you want everyone to think you're perfect," I snapped. "In doing so, not only did you besmirch my mother's memory, you shook my faith in her and made me question my own abilities. What you did was mean-spirited at best, and you know it. That's why you were always hanging around. You were trying to make up for Mother's death. Being around us also gave you an opportunity to find some way to keep me as far away from airplanes as possible. You knew that if I flew and my experience as a pilot grew, I'd start to question what had really happened. So you offered to send me to—of all places!—charm school."

Wilbert studied me very closely. I imagined that he was trying to decide if he could somehow get me to keep his secret. "So what do you propose to do?"

"I intend to tell the world that you were piloting that plane."

He scoffed. "How are you going to do that? This isn't exactly headline material."

"Mr. Byrd, a newspaper reporter, is doing a series of articles about the ferrying program. One of the people being interviewed in great detail is me. I intend to set the record straight, and since Mr. Byrd's articles are going to appear all over the country, it won't be long before everyone knows what you did."

"Liz, please. Think about what you're doing."

"I've thought about it a lot. My mother's memory will be redeemed, and you'll be known for the rat that you are. You should have died in that plane crash, not Mother. After all, it was your idea to fly into the storm that day. Telling the truth is not the perfect ending; the perfect ending would be to see Mother walk through the door. Telling the truth doesn't bring about perfect justice either, but it's a start."

Wilbert opened his mouth to say something, then for only the second time that I could ever remember, became speechless. He simply stared at the floor.

I rose, put the letter into my purse, patted the locket that hung around my neck, and walked out of room 226. I had accomplished what at one time I thought was impossible to do and ended a major chapter in my life.

Chapter 18

As Father, Joe, Mr. Byrd, and I, James Edwin Erickson,
an up-and-coming young actor, waited in the hallway
outside the room where Liz's graduation ceremony was to
be held, I could hardly contain my excitement. I hadn't
seen my sister for more than four months, and there was
so much to talk about and so many dreams to share.

To pass the time until the graduates arrived, I studied
the people around me. Father was so happy and so
different from the man he had been for the last month
that I could hardly believe my eyes. He smiled, nodded to
passersby in the hall, and visited with Joe and Mr. Byrd.
Father's clothes were rumpled as usual, for clothing—in
fact, appearance in general—has never been very
important to him. From time to time, he examined and
re-examined the formal graduation invitation in his hand,

running his fingers over the heavy vellum and engraved letters.

When I looked at Joe, I couldn't help smiling. You would have thought that he was about to receive the highest award ever given in the whole world and that everyone would be watching. Joe was very nervous, and he constantly checked his appearance in a nearby window. Each time he did so, he adjusted his tie and pulled down the sleeves on his dark blue suit jacket—the first that I'd ever seen him wear. He seemed to think that the sleeves were too short. He also repeatedly smoothed down his hair. It didn't do much good, though. Strands would pop up again in only a few minutes.

Mr. Byrd, on the other hand, was calm. His gray pin-striped suit looked very professional, and I thought that such a suit might look better on me than the tan outfit I was wearing and had nearly outgrown. He carried a notepad, several fountain pens, and an impressive camera with a big flash bulb. Mr. Byrd and Father had talked about the camera in detail for what seemed like an eternity. Father's thinking about getting one just like it for the *Telegram*.

When I got tired of watching people, I paced back and forth in the hall. I now was certain that the students would never ever appear.

But I was wrong. At long last, the graduates arrived. When Liz saw us, she broke from her group and ran to us. We took turns hugging her and offering her our most heartfelt congratulations. She looked great, even though she was wearing a strange-looking hat. Liz was really thin now, but when she put her arms around us, she seemed stronger than ever before—a result, no doubt, of the many push-ups that she's done since her arrival in Texas.

When all of the "hellos" were over, Liz stepped back and surveyed the group. "Uncle Wilbert?" she asked cautiously.

Father smiled a little and shook his head. "Wilbert left a message at the desk. He said that there was an emergency in his office and that he had to return to Chicago as quickly as possible." Now Father grinned as he looked at Liz. "Wilbert didn't even say good-bye."

"I wouldn't have said good-bye, either," I replied. "After all, he must have realized that we'd eventually find out about what happened in room 226 last night. How could he possibly face any of us after that?"

Liz looked at me. "How do you know what happened last night?" she asked.

"I was in room 224," I replied, "and I just happened to overhear a rather loud conversation."

"It was not loud!" Liz said.

"Loud enough," I replied. "I could hear every word." I then pulled out my journal and began to read from my notes, changing my voice as needed to indicate two speakers. " 'This isn't a social call, Uncle Wilbert . . . I intend to tell the world that you were piloting that plane . . .' 'Liz, please. Think about what you're doing . . .' 'I've thought about it a lot. My mother's memory will be redeemed, and you'll be known for the weasel that you are—' "

"Rat," Liz said, interrupting me. "I called him a rat." She stared at me, wide-eyed and a little shocked. "I can't believe that you listened to the whole thing."

"You were great," I said, "really great. I wasn't about to walk away from one of the best scenes that I've ever witnessed. Besides, Father listened too."

Liz gasped. "Father? The same Father that's punished you at least one hundred times for eavesdropping?" She turned to look at him, her eyes even wider than before.

Father actually blushed a little as he nodded his head. "I listened to you and Wilbert. You can take my favorite radio programs away for a week as a punishment. I'm not proud of what I did, listening to a private conversation, but I am glad that I heard what you said." He took a deep breath. "When we got the letter from the clinic, I thought that your mother might have deliberately flown into the storm to . . . to . . ."

When Father looked away and I knew that he couldn't say the rest, I finished for him. "To die."

Liz's expression was somber now, and she chose her words carefully. "Mother would have been upset, and she might have thought about dying immediately rather than facing a long and losing struggle with diabetes as her father and Aunt Levina had. But Mother never—*never!*— would have endangered another life, not even that of Uncle Wilbert, who sometimes made her very angry."

Joe, who had known Mother well, nodded in agreement.

Father's eyes misted over. "You have no idea how many

120

times I have told myself that she wouldn't . . . but I didn't have any proof. And then you confronted Wilbert—"

"Liz! We need to get in line," a very pretty lady with long brown hair and a southern accent called out as she motioned to my sister.

Liz hugged Father once more. "Everything's all right now," she said softly. She stepped back, looked at each of us in turn and smiled. "I've got to go. I'll meet you right here after the ceremony."

While the graduates lined up in the hall, we entered the room set aside for the graduation, and Father, Joe, and I took our assigned seats, just right of the center aisle in the seventh row. Mr. Byrd decided to remain in the back of the room, a good vantage point, he said, for taking photos during the program.

Even though this was a typical lecture room, it looked anything but ordinary tonight. A dozen American flags on gold poles outlined the back of what served as a stage: a large wooden platform with steps on the left and right. Red pleated fabric hung from the stage to the floor, and two huge white baskets stuffed with dozens of red carnations flanked the dark oak speaker's stand, which stood front and center in the spotlight. Behind the podium three empty chairs and a table, draped in red-white-and-blue fabric and topped with what I guessed to be certificates and silver wings, faced the audience. In addition, red, white, and blue banners were draped over seventeen chairs in the front row where Liz and her classmates would sit.

The program started at exactly eight o'clock. It began with graduates, shoulders back and heads held erect, walking down the center aisle. We rose when they entered the room to show our respect, and we remained standing until the women were seated. General Arnold and Jackie Cochran then took their seats behind the speaker's stand while Major Hogan approached the podium. After a brief welcome by the major, we sang the national anthem and recited the Pledge of Allegiance. These events were followed by a long speech about sacrifice by General Arnold, a brief history of the program by Jackie Cochran, and a lot of flashes of light as Mr. Byrd recorded the event on film.

One hour later, we finally got to the important part: handing out the certificates. One by one, Arnold called out the graduates' names, "Cox . . . Dixon . . . Erickson." As he did so, they rose, climbed the steps, and walked to the podium.

When General Arnold pinned a pair of wings on my sister, the gold stars on his shoulder gleamed in the spotlight. Liz had always said that she had wanted to touch the stars, and when she shook hands with the general and then Mrs. Cochran, in a way Liz had done so. And when Arnold shook hands with Liz, he too had touched a star, a star with an especially bright future.

Afterword

To Touch the Stars is based on actual events. Young women really did ferry planes during World War II for the army air force. Many would-be pilots, like the heroine of this story, saw ferrying as both a great way to help the war effort and start a career in aviation. More than 25,000 women applied for training; 1,830 were accepted, and of those, only 1,074 received their wings. At the beginning of the war, women had to be at least 21 years old and have a minimum of 500 hours of flight time to apply, but as the need for pilots grew, women as young as 18 were admitted. What really mattered was not age, but the women's skills and their willingness to work hard and learn the army way.

Word spread quickly throughout the army air force about hundreds of beautiful young women training at

Avenger Airfield. Shortly after, so many pilots requested permission to make "emergency" landings at the base, that it had to be declared off-limits to all except the students, their instructors, and support staff.

Planes used during training sessions were, on occasion, tampered with, and the incidents described in this book—an engine fire and severed cables—actually happened. Some of the incidents were reported to Cochran; none were reported to General Henry Arnold, since both the students and Cochran believed that an investigation would shut down the program. Instead, the women took their chances. The culprits were never identified.

After graduation, pilots performed a number of tasks. Most ferried planes. Female pilots delivered 75 percent of the aircraft used during the war, logging more than 60 million miles while doing so. Some of these planes were experimental, and the women who flew these aircraft received special training in bearing sidearms and marksmanship to enable them to protect their planes from enemy spies if need be. Other women delivered cargo, tested aircraft, and towed targets behind their planes so soldiers on the ground could practice shooting at moving objects in the sky. Some even practiced evasive action at night to give ground crews experience in finding, spotlighting, and targeting enemy bombers.

The jobs that the women performed were not without risk. Thirty-eight died during the war, including Cornelia Fort. At least one of these deaths was blamed on a vandalized plane; upon investigation, Cochran found large amounts of sugar in the gas tank.

In late 1943, Nancy Love's and Jackie Cochran's organizations merged, and the new group was called the Women's Airforce Service Pilots. Members were known as WASPs, and it is these women who are often thought of when female ferrying pilots come to mind, even though they had numerous predecessors. WASP was headed by Cochran.

When the war began to wind down in late 1944, the demand for ferrying pilots decreased dramatically. Female pilots were the first to be relieved of their jobs, even though some offered to fly for the army air force until the end of the war for a dollar.

For many years, the contributions of female ferrying pilots were all but forgotten. In fact, in 1976 when the air force, by then a separate branch in the armed services, decided to train women to fly and the government released a statement saying that the women accepted for the program would be the first women in American history to fly for the military, former WASPs were deeply upset. What about us? they asked. Doesn't anyone remember what we did?

To make sure that they would not be forgotten, the WASPs, along with Colonel Bruce Arnold, son of General Henry Arnold, and Senator Barry Goldwater, who had also ferried planes during the war, decided to push for formal recognition. After some heated debates in Congress in 1977, the federal government officially recognized the role that female pilots had played in the war effort and the many contributions they had made as support staff for the armed services. The women were not given veterans' benefits or status, though, which several supporters had fought for in Congress. However, the women's hard work was at least formally and very publicly acknowledged.

On May 22, 1993, a memorial was dedicated to these women at Avenger Field, which is now the site of Texas State Technical College. Two long, black granite walls flank a walkway, the Walk of Honor, that leads to a shallow wishing pool. The names of all trainees have been chiseled into the stone, and gold stars mark the names of the women who died during training or ferrying activities. In the middle of the pool is a life-sized bronze statue of a ferrying pilot in oversized coveralls. This statue was created by a former WASP, Dorothy Swain Lewis. The WASP motto is also proudly displayed at the memorial: "We Live in the Wind and the Sand, and Our Eyes Are on the Stars," a motto Liz would have loved.

Entrance to Aviation Enterprises, WASP flight training at Avenger Field,
Sweetwater, Texas

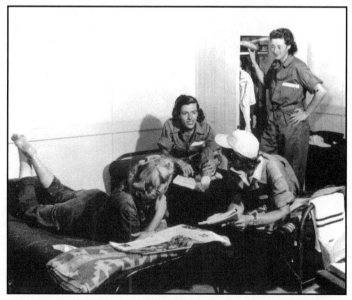

WASP trainees in their quarters, called "bays"

WASP trainees being briefed in the ready room before flight, Avenger Field

WASPs head for primary training in Stearman PT-13s, Avenger Field, 1943

WASP trainees study flight plans at Perrin Army Air Base, Sherman, Texas, 1944

WASP Ellen Gery prepares to ferry a UC-64 from Montreal, Quebec to Savannah, Georgia, August 1944

Inspection of WASP detachment by Jacqueline Cochran and Brigadier General Stearley at Camp Davis Army Air Field, North Carolina

General Hap Arnold hands out silver wings to the last graduating class of WASPs, December 7, 1944.